ANTHONY G. M

THE
RECKLESS
ANTICS
OF THE
PURDY STREET
GANG

outskirts
press

Outskirts Press, Inc.
http://www.outskirtspress.com

ISBN: 978-1-9772-3367-7

US Copyright Registration Number: TXu 2-214-437

Cover Illustration © 2021 Outskirts Press, Inc.. All rights reserved - used with permission.

Outskirts Press and the "OP" logo are trademarks belonging to Outskirts Press, Inc.

PRINTED IN THE UNITED STATES OF AMERICA

This book is dedicated to my wife Pat for the countless hours she spent with me. Only love can endure the trials of an author husband. Without her support I would never have reached the point of publication.

And to the memory of my good childhood friends Marco and Michael Bisceglia, and Frank Sollazzo that I had the good fortune to meet with and relive those days once again in our Golden Years before they left us in 2019 and 2020.

To my brother Michael who helped us get through the tough times in our early years. He passed in 2016.

To my mother who exemplified strength, fairness and love of family above everything else.

To Bobby Sollazzo for sharing his memories of those adventurous days in "The Purdy Street Gang."

Finally, to my brother John who always challenged and encouraged me to go beyond mediocrity.

This work depicts actual events in the life of the author as truthfully as recollection permits.

This is a book of memory, and memory has its own tale to tell. But I have done my best to make it tell a truthful story.

Table of Contents

MAP

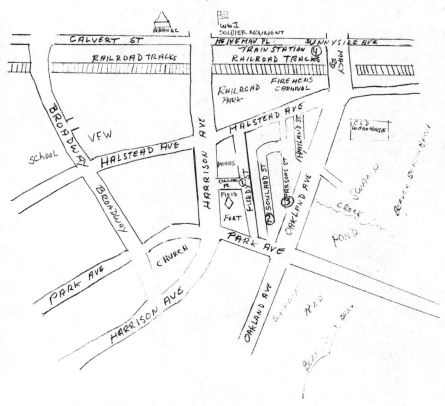

① SOLLAZZO APARTMENT
② BISCEGLIA HOUSE
③ MATEROS HOUSE

ONE

"IS EVERYTHING THE WAY YOU REMEMBERED?"

On a visit to my daughter's home in Katonah, New York, I decided it was time for me to tell my story of times long ago-the days of childhood and early adolescence.

As I drove, my heart raced with anticipation and the excitement of seeing the old neighborhood. Within a half a square mile, the world (as we knew it) was comprised of twelve streets, divided by Harrison Avenue, a major thoroughfare: Oakland Avenue, Macy Road, and the marshes on the east; the New Haven Railroad tracks, Heineman Place, and Sunnyside Avenue on the north; Halstead Avenue on the west; and Broadway and Park Avenue on the south. They formed the border for the remaining five streets: Parsons, Soulard, Purdy, Fremont Street, and Archer Place. Each of these streets has a storied history of our adventures as The Purdy Street Gang.

Accompanying me on that drive was a constant memory of the happiest and most vivid memories of those days in 1951 when we played on the Purdy Street field and of the mischievous times we had in the surrounding neighborhoods of Harrison, New York.

Upon arriving at Purdy Street, I parked the car. I was stunned. The open field I so coveted is now a blacktop parking lot. I felt the memories of yesterday, crushed and sealed forever under the weight of the blacktop. I walked down the street. What was once our "mountain" had been demolished and replaced by a barracks-style brick and stucco-coated two-story building, now silencing the cries we made on top of that high point as we yelled, "Tarzan!" or snuffed out small fires with branches to mimic Indian smoke signals that warned of cavalry or cowboys approaching. As I scanned the front and side of the building, I saw an open space and wooded area.

Entering the building, I approached the young women in the office and requested permission to see the back yard. "Miss, I'm here visiting some relatives up north. My reason for stopping in is to get your permission to see the back property. You see, where your building is constructed, there was once a rock formation with a cave and, behind it, was an area where my friends and I built a fort when we were kids. I would just like to go there and get a sense of time long past.

She chuckled, probably thinking this old guy wants to relive his past. "Sure. Go ahead."

Behind the building was a lawn that went to the chain link fence bordering the old Protestant cemetery, the last vestiges of the field I remembered. This small parcel of land was one of the most important parts of those adolescent years. I looked down at the grass in disappointment that everything had changed.

When I went back to the office to thank the young woman, she folded cupped her hands and rested her chin on them and then, with a look of concern, asked, "Is everything the way you remembered?"

"No. Unfortunately it is not. Thank you."

Dispirited, I went back to my car. Leaning against it, arms tightly crossed over my chest, I tried very hard to comfort myself over the disappoint-ments in the field, deeply feeling a sense of loss that the times shared here were truly gone forever. Other children could not enjoy it in some of the ways my friends and I did.

TWO

"I DON'T LIKE THIS PLACE; IT LOOKS MEAN"

I often think back to how close we were as friends. Our families never socialized, but we were constantly with one another like a family of brothers without the parental overseeing. I think the reason we related to one another is because we had a common bond. Our families migrated from Southern Italy in the early 1900's when millions of Italians left Italy to better their lives in America.

Myself, my brother Johnny, Marco and Michael were first generation. My parents' families migrated from the towns of Maddolni and Sant'Agata Dé Goti, in Benevento and Casserta Province Italy. Both my grandfathers came first, around 1903, eventually bringing their families. My mother and father's families finally were united around 1910.

Marco and Michael Bisceglia's family came from Terlizzi in the Apulia Region. Their father Patsy arrived with his family in 1902 at the age of 9. Their mother, Teresa, came with her family in 1918 after World War One.

Bobby and Frank Sollazzo's families were second generation.

Marco, Michael, Bobby and Frank's families were better off financially than we were. Marco and Michael's father established a successful plaster and stucco business. Frank and Bobby's father was a successful coach and headed up the Aranac, the town's recreation center. Their families were frugal. I don't remember Bobby, Frank, Marco or Michael having pocket change for the movies or other things.

Our family's financial resources were dependent on social security and county assistance after my father passed away in 1945.

> It was mid-May. I was three months shy of my 4th birthday, Johnny was six, and our oldest brother Michael, who went by the name Sonny, was nine. The memory of that day is seared into my brain with details sharper than what might be expected of a child's recollection.

It was a warm, sunlit day. The flowers in our yard were sprouting spectacular colors of iris purple, daffodil yellow, and tulip red. The beautiful lilac bushes nestled along each side of our house, added their strong sweet fragrance to the kaleidoscope of flowers. The trees were in full bloom, filtering the sun's molten gold rays, which were so strong that I squinted my eyes each time I looked up to the branches where the robins and sparrows perched on their limbs. It was a time to daydream with nature's wonderful attractions.

My mother called out, "Hurry up, Anthony! Get dressed. We have to catch the bus."

I turned to utter an objection. Then I remembered that we were going to the hospital to see my father. It had been a month since I'd seen him. When he left for the hospital, sick with bleeding ulcers, my Aunt Rosie and Uncle Joe had to help him to the car. Mom told us they were taking him to the hospital for an operation that would make him feel better. Then one day, my mother told us that he was getting weaker and wanted to see us.

I was confused. I thought he was going to get better.

Looking at the dark circles under my mother's eyes and hearing the uncompromising command left me with a very bad feeling.

As we left the house through the side door, the sun's rays pierced the two kitchen windows over the sink, splitting the window grate into a series of shadows shaped like crosses on the linoleum floor. Mom turned around before opening the door and paused for one moment, looking at them with something like finality. She was a religious person, and the crosses on the linoleum floor may have been a grim omen of the personal suffering she would endure without my father. Did she know he was going to die soon? Was she afraid of the future and what it held for her, alone with three young children?

Once outside, my mother pulled me at a brisk pace up Parsons Street to the bus stop on Halstead Avenue. "Hurry, Anthony. Stop dragging your feet."

But I dug in. I didn't want to go. I didn't like the tense feeling my mother was conveying. I wanted to be home playing in the yard with my brothers and watching the birds in the trees.

Her grip was tight as she pulled me along. I wanted to miss the bus. I was afraid that when we got to the hospital, my father would be gone.

My brothers were yelling at me because I was causing so much trouble for my mother. Sonny was so upset with me that he raised his fist in anger and was about to punch me. But I hid behind my mother.

Then Johnny ended it with a bribe. "Anthony, we're gonna go on a big bus today for a long ride. And after that, we're gonna have ice cream." The ice cream was a lie. He had a habit of doing this, but it did the trick and calmed me down.

At the bus stop on Halstead Avenue, I felt better. People were shopping, cars were whizzing by, trains were clacking noise on the the New York/New Haven railroad steel tracks that ran parallel to Halstead Avenue. Behind the bus stop and all along Halstead Avenue were four-story apartment buildings with street level stores. Women were shopping for their families. They left each store with their arms filled with groceries, laundry, or clothes from the tailor shop. At my young age, I thought it was magic for anyone who entered the stores, thinking they were rewarded with something to take home.

Behind the bus stop was an Italian delicatessen with cylinder-shaped cheeses wrapped with string and hanging from hooks in the window. All I could think of was eating some of the cheese or having a dish of macaroni and spreading parmesan on it. Next to the delicatessen was a Chinese laundry, its front windows foggy with steam. Each time the door opened, puffs of finger-like white steam followed the customers as if to grab them and prevent them from leaving. In the window, a man pushed down on a dry-clean press, never looking up. Each time he pulled down on the press, my head went down. When he pulled up, my head went up. My brother Johnny stared at him as well and imitated the man's expressions each time he pressed down on the lever. Johnny squinted his eyes like an Asian and made faces. If my mother had seen him do it, she would have whacked him across the head. Sonny was quiet, just watching over us.

My brothers and mother kept looking to their left for the bus. I couldn't see anything but the cars and people whizzing by. Then out of nowhere, this big blue and silver bus appeared. My heart raced with joy.

A pleasing smile came to my mother's face. She touched my nose with a soft tap of her finger as she looked down at me. Her dark brown eyes had a serene look, much like they did before my father got sick. Her black hair was neat and silky, and she was wearing a simple floral-patterned dress that she had made. She sensed my happy anticipation of the bus ride and, for a brief moment, she was Mom again.

The driver watched as my mother lifted me up the steps. Wow! The steering wheel looked like a big skinny truck wheel with spokes in it. I was fascinated and wondered how the driver could turn such a big wheel. Then he grabbed a lever that pulled the doors shut with a scissor-like device. The awe on my face invoked a smile from him.

My brothers sat silently in the seat in front of us, which was unusual for Johnny, though not so unusual for our older brother Sonny who was normally quiet, yet this day even more so. It bothered me that he was saying so little this whole trip.

I sat to the right of my mother in the seat next to the open window. As the bus picked up speed, the warm May breeze tickled my face and rustled my hair. It was such a good feeling that I stuck my arm out to feel the breeze press against my palm and filter through my fingers.

"Anthony! Get your hand inside!" My mother grabbed my arm with force and pulled it in. Eyes narrowed and forehead creased, she once again had a look of anguish on her face. "You could have lost your arm if a truck came by too close to the bus!" That look—Oh, how uncomfortable it made me.

The rest of the ride was mostly silent. At each stop, as the driver opened the door, I lifted my head up to see who was getting on and off. I loved watching people pull the bell cord to stop the bus. The doors, when opened and closed, emitted a nerve-jolting screech, followed by the noise of the motor accelerating as the bus moved away from the stop. It seemed we would never get to the hospital.

We finally arrived at the United Hospital bus stop. The adventure of the bus ride was gone, and the earlier fear returned. My mother nudged me off the bus onto the sidewalk. As the vehicle pulled away, it belched black smoke into our faces.

"Oh, what a smell," Mom cried out. And, although I choked and almost vomited from the slimy taste of the smoke, my brothers were oblivious.

Before crossing the street, Mom grasped my left hand and ordered Sonny, "Grab Johnny's hand and mine. Don't cross the street until I tell you." Looking left to right for oncoming traffic, she uttered the command, "Go," and we dashed across the street. My mother and my brothers were moving so fast I could just about keep up with them. I thought for sure I was going to trip and get hit by a car.

On the hospital side of the street, we released our hands. In front of us was the winding concrete walkway forming an S-shape that gradually sloped upward to the hospital, a block-shaped, dark-brown brick building sitting on top of a hill. Trees bordered the landscaped grounds. We stood there silent, staring, quietly anticipating what was waiting for us. Johnny and Sonny looked at Mom, waiting for the signal from her to walk. But Mom seemed frozen. I was looking at my brothers' worried facial expressions. Just then a passing car horn honked, startling her into movement.

At the main doors, my mother turned toward us, her expression one of distress and despondency. She crouched toward me and my brother Johnny with her lips clenched, holding back her emotions. "You can't go to your father's room. The hospital won't let children under twelve visit," she said sadly. "Sonny will take you to the fire escape where you can climb to your father's room and sit outside the window."

My brother Johnny and I looked at each other, confused. Looking back. I realized why Sonny was so quiet on the bus. He knew we wouldn't be allowed to see our father.

I wanted to see Dad, to touch him, and to give him a hug. Not being able to do so sent a surge of confusion and hurt into me. My heart felt like a spear was thrust into it. Tears were slowly dripping down my face, leaking the hurt I felt. Johnny pulled on Mom's blouse sleeve angrily shouting with tears streaking down his face, "Mom, it's not fair! We want to see him. Please let us go with you."

My mother grabbed both of us, pulling us tightly against her as we cried.

We left my mother and started toward the fire escape, my brothers each holding one of my hands. When we got to the fire escape I craned my neck and stared up at the metal grate floor, steel ladder, and railing. The ladder and the steps beyond it looked like a stairway to the clouds. The fire escape was painted black and bolted into the brick of the building. I became apprehensive that, if I got on it, I could fall. Maybe that's why there was no one else climbing it—they all fell and never would return.

Sonny hoisted my brother Johnny onto the ladder and then lifted me up. I held the slippery rungs tightly, afraid that I would fall at any moment. My brother Johnny coaxed me to move up the ladder. "C'mon, Anthony, you can do it! Grab one bar at a time."

Little by little, I moved up to my brother, my hands grabbing the rungs, holding them tightly, fearful of falling. Once there, I felt a sense of relief, only to find out that we had to move up the steps to the second-floor window where my father's room was.

I was about to cry when Sonny came up to me. "Anthony, you want to see Daddy, don't you?"

I nodded yes, but started to cry again, pointing to the hallway where doctors wearing masks were walking. "I don't like this place. It looks mean."

Sonny pulled me up. "C'mon, Anthony, I'll stay with you," and we went up the fire escape toward my father's window.

Each step was an eternity. My brothers held me because I felt for sure my legs would go through the space between steps and cast me down. Finally, we arrived. The curtains were drawn back so we could see my father who was sitting up in bed.

The window was open far enough that we could hear the voices of our mother and relatives.

But not a sound was coming from my father. He stared at the wall, motionless.

My brothers called to him, but I don't remember uttering any words myself. All I remember is my mother taking my father's hand as if to wake him up and pointing her free hand to the window as he looked up at her.

Slowly, he turned to look at us. He smiled. Then he lifted his left arm weakly, struggling to raise it enough to wave.

It wasn't long after that visit that my father died. Memorial Day.

> *The only memory of my father alive is carved into that day when my brothers and I stood outside the window of the hospital. The feeling of hopelessness and loss that was to be our legacy for some time entered our lives at an early age. It was displayed to us in full view when they laid my father out in our home which was the tradition back then.*

I went to the casket and stood on the prayer kneeler to peer at my father with the rosary wrapped around his hands, motionless, not responding to my calls. Then I touched his hands. The coldness of them frightened me.

My father's friend—I can only remember his name as Sam—saw this and pulled me off the kneeler. Gently he held my arms and said, "Anthony, Daddy can't talk. He's in Heaven. You have to be strong for your mom." Funny thing, Sam looked a lot like my father. It was almost as if my father was talking to me.

My brothers and I were so overwhelmed with my father's death that we were unable to express our hurt, anger, and feeling of abandonment. In particular, my brother Johnny, angry at my father's death, was determined that my father would not leave the house. The day of the funeral, as my mother was gathering us up for the ride to the cemetery, he couldn't be found. My mother kept calling out for him, becoming increasingly worried that something had happened to him. Everyone went out looking for him. My Uncle Tony found him.

Holding Johnny by the back of the collar, my uncle gave my mother a stern look of disapproval. "Rose, he let the air out of the tires on all the cars."

Frustrated, distraught, and embarrassed, Mom gave Johnny a hard slap to his buttocks.

Johnny, his chin tucked against his chest, tears streaming, cried, "I don't want them to take Daddy away!"

Temporarily, he succeeded. The hearse and all the relatives' and friends' cars had one or more flat tires. Every one of the men had to get air pumps to fill them. It was a hot day, and they were sweating. We could hear them cursing under their breaths in Italian. By the time they were finished, their Sunday clothes were all rumpled from perspiration and stained with tire dirt.

At this point in our lives, we felt the tragic hopelessness of losing our father. The loss was real. Our father's death gave us a sober understanding at an early age of life's disappointments and how important it was to overcome adversity. To achieve our goals, we had to operate without the guidance of a father.

Our early friendship with Marco, Michael, Bobby, and Frank was a positive experience in our lives. In many situations, we were guided by their experiences with *their* fathers. Even with this interaction, our friends, my brothers, and I learned by trial and error the consequences of our decisions.

THREE

"I GUESS YOU'RE CHICKENS AND QUITTERS."

We were called "The Purdy Street Gang." The core of the gang was made up of six brothers from three Italian-American families: Anthony and Johnny Matero, Michael and Marco Bisceglia, and Frank and Bobby Sollazzo. The younger brothers Anthony (me), Michael, and Bobby were ten years old. The older brothers Johnny and Marco were twelve, and Frank thirteen. We had an impenetrable bond, our personalities merged into one family of brothers.

We got that name because we always met at this field that was once an open rectangular lot bordering Purdy Street, Colonial Street, and Park Ave. This lot was the catalyst for our imaginary worlds where we became great baseball players in the major leagues and football players for our high school team. It was also our meeting place where we conspired mischievous activities, alarming neighbors and parents with our daring exploits.

The lot was mostly a level field of knee-high rye grass that stretched from the edge of Colonial Street and traversed to the rock and cave formation we called "The Mountain" on Purdy Street and inclining to Park Ave. The mountain was about fifteen feet high and forty feet long and twenty-five feet wide. Within it was a narrow cave four-foot wide, about six-foot high, and ran eight feet deep. Behind it the open field continued to a wooded area eventually ending at a chain link fence. On the other side of the chain link fence was the small eighteenth-century cemetery overgrown at that time with vines choking the tombstones that had fallen to the ground and wild bushes hiding the standing tombstones. We used to clear the front of the field facing Colonial and the side of it facing Purdy Street. We cut the knee-high grass with scythes that we got from Mr. Bisceglias' tool shed, until the field was shaped like a baseball field in the summer. Baseball and football in the fall was the glue that brought the gang together.

In the winter months we would migrate to the marshes, today known as Beaver Preserve and to the Frank P. Sollazzo Recreation Center, in our time known as the Aranac.

As I was reminiscing, I heard a child's playful voice coming somewhere from the apartment building across the street. I looked up and saw that building where my friends Bobby and Frank Sollazzo once lived.

It is unchanged from the time of my youth—a three-story high apartment building with a field stone and stucco façade just as it was then. Shifting my eyes to the right of the building, where there was once a hill and pathway from Soulard Street, I envisioned the faces of Marco and Michael Bisceglia, as well as my brother Johnny and I, jostling with each other as we walked up the hill and met Frank and Bobby on our way to school or to hang around in the neighborhood.

Johnny met Marco and Frank when they went to kindergarten. Establishing that early friendship eventually brought me, Michael, and Bobby into their circle. The bonds grew stronger as we continued on to the higher grades in Halstead Avenue school renamed Parsons Memorial School.

Often we planned to meet at the field to play pickup baseball or football. Sometimes weather conditions would prevent us from doing so and forced us indoors. The boredom of staying indoors with nothing to do drove us crazy.

To offset the boredom, we needed the companionship of one another. We did this by hanging out in the neighborhood. We loved to shoot the breeze and share each other's comic books while hanging around in the hallway of the Sollazzo apartment building, our voices bouncing off the walls of the hallway and echoing our conversations or running up and down the steps driving the apartment dwellers to open their doors to tell us to keep quiet. There were only so many games of checkers to play or comic books to read. This was long before the wonders of today's technology.

One day after school in late April, we met at the Sollazzo's apartment building. We gathered around the front steps in a semicircle. It was a warm spring day, and we all had our sweaters and jackets looped over our arms or on our laps. The warm weather got us talking about the days remaining until summer vacation and, of course, the impending baseball season.

I was sitting on the steps, arms folded across my chest in the ready position like a judo expert. "We have forty more days until school is out." I jumped up with a smile. "I can't wait to get out and play ball every day!"

I used to like busting Bobby's chops about the rivalry between the Dodgers and Yankees baiting him to respond with something like this "Yogi Berra and Joe DiMaggio won't help the Yankees this year because Duke Snider and Roy Campanella will outhit them!"

When it came to the Yankees, Bobby tended to get a little excited. The mere mention of the Dodgers beating the Yankees would provoke him. With his face in mine, he stood so close that I could see the spacing between his two front teeth. Bobby was overweight but very strong, measuring about five feet two and weighing 145 pounds. Despite his mass, he was quick on his feet. He would come at me like a **bull whenever I agitated him, ready to fight, his chest leaning forward, arms in front and hands clutched into fists** ready to punch the living daylights out of me, **knocking me off balance.** He took any opportunity he had to prove he was the strongest.

Whenever I sensed his attack mode, I got the hell out of his way before he went ballistic. Compared to Bobby, I was lighter at only 95 pounds and shorter at 4'11," strong but not as strong as him or some of the others.

A few of the guys supported my position, but not everyone. It was clear that the gang was divided on who was or wasn't going to win.

Michael, when he saw others like Bobby threaten me, would jump in front of me to protect me. Michael was built like a bulldog. Shorter than me by one inch or Bobby by five inches, Michael could lift either of us up and throw us down. He had well-developed muscles. When he punched, the pain from the impact would cause a person to howl in agony. His curly head looked like a volleyball with hair. He used that head when fighting, going for the mid-section of his opponent, then pummeled them with punches. He had courage that I envied. People often thought we were brothers because of our fair complexions and blond hair, but he was my best friend and always came to my aid whenever someone threatened me.

Michael and I became best friends before we went to kindergarten. We lived one block from one another. He lived on Soulard Street, and I lived on Parsons street. One day when I was playing by myself in the yard, I looked up to a natural stone hill across the street that I used to think really was a mountain. Standing on top of the "mountain" was Michael waving to me to come up. I dropped my toy metal dump truck and left the yard to meet him.

I thought to myself that he had a big head.

The first thing he said was, "Do you want to play with me?"

From then on, we would play together every day.

One time he invited me to his home after kindergarten class. He pulled out a box of what we thought were cookies and started eating them. Neither one of us knew how to read at the time. Mrs. Bisceglia, his mom, walked in, and her sweet smile turned to horror. "Maddona mia!" She pulled what we thought were cookies out of hands. We must have eaten two of them each before she stopped us from eating more. Her sweet smile returned and, in a very caring way, she explained, "You can't eat these; they're biscuits for the dog!" Michael and I spit out what was still in our mouths.

Often when the gang had disagreements, their aggressive nature would come to the forefront. Depending on the issue, they would nudge and push each other to the point of exchanging blows. For example, like the discussion I had with Bobby on the Yankees vs the Dodgers. When that happened, Frank or Johnny would silence everyone.

But Frank, as the biggest of all the guys and with a heavy-set frame of five feet six inches and shoulders like a pro football lineman, commanded our respect in heated disputes and silenced the gang. He had a habit of blowing the drooping black hair out of his eyes, especially in the summer. His complexion was fair similar to Bobby's. Both he and Bobby looked more Irish than Southern Italian. He loved sports and always wanted to play sandlot ball. His love and knowledge of sports came from his father who taught us the importance of each playing position in baseball and football and reading the sports section of the New York Daily News. We loved reading the stats on the major league team players.

When Frank roared like a lion, the gang became very quiet. You didn't challenge him. Otherwise, you risked a confrontation with him. He was overly defensive when challenged. Whenever he told everyone to shut up, the only sounds heard were cars whooshing on Purdy Street and the wind moving the high grass in the field.

My brother Johnny asked everyone that April day what they were planning for the summer. He wanted to do different things during those months, and not always play sandlot ball.

We were confused by what he meant "do different things." In addition to playing sand lot ball, our summer routine involved riding our bikes for about three miles to the next town, Rye, New York, where we would go swimming at Oakland Beach and roam the boardwalk of Playland amusement park. And we played in the marshes across the street from our house in what is known today as *Beaver Swamp Wetlands*, swinging from willow trees, rafting the creeks and pond with three by three-foot rafts made with flat boards and thick tree branches

Johnny suggesting a change in our summer routine received untrustworthy looks and a chorus of expletives.

My brother Johnny was the instigator and head of the gang. He was quite effective in outthinking the two older brothers, resulting in him becoming the default leader. Compared to Frank, he was smaller in height and build, yet bigger than Marco by two inches. He had thick black hair and an olive complexion. I often wondered how he was able to manipulate Frank since he was three inches shorter than Frank. But he was a fighter. And if anyone challenged him, he was quick to go against the challenger. My older brother, Sonny and I could get him excited by sometimes calling him "Skinny." Hearing that name, he would do one of two things—pounce on you, punching your upper arm that hurt so much afterward that you could barely move it, or he would walk away resenting what you said and not speak to you for days and sometimes weeks. Not speaking to you held more dangerous connotations than a direct punch. He harbored his angry thoughts sometimes waiting for the opportunity to use them in reprisal when you least expected. Often his detractors would back down from him.

Confrontation and daring were definitely not qualities he lacked. If he had an idea, he was quite pushy, like a gnat constantly around you. He could be the most charming, compassionate, and loving person in one moment and, at other times, be the meanest, harsh, and critical person. You had to be able to navigate between his moods. He always stood up for me whether I was right or wrong. But when I was wrong, he would tell me later in private.

He had strong leadership qualities. Sometimes for the good, and sometimes for the bad. But he was able to motivate us to achieve levels at an early age that most boys did not achieve until their late teen and adult years.

Despite being smaller and leaner than Frank, Johnny was never one to shy away from a confrontation with him. He was forceful with his ideas and assumed the leadership role of the gang. Whenever he did so, his face would crinkle, eyes narrow, and lips tightened, driving home his point. He was effective in controlling us. He loved to be challenged to prove his points.

That April day with a branch in hand, Johnny motioned everyone off the steps to the Purdy Street field across the street from the Sollazo brothers' apartment building. He had us form a circle at the makeshift home plate, casting aside the carboard home plate, knelt down on his right knee and drew a rectangular box in the dirt.

Then he put the stick down, stood up, turned toward us, and before anyone could question him, he picked up the stick again, and with the words that would change our lives that summer and forever be in our memories.

I remember his words: "Ever since we saw the movie, *Fort Apache*, and heard about the Crusades during religious instruction, I've been thinking of building a fort like this."

Our mouths dropped.

Pointing with his right index finger, he said, "We can build the fort right there in that corner of the field where the trees can prevent anyone seeing it" pointing his hand toward the knoll in front the old Presbyterian cemetery. "And the cave on Purdy Street will protect the front."

Looking at the drawing, the gang still were not convinced that a fort could be built where he pointed. Especially since the old cemetery was separated from the field by a chain link fence. They were afraid of being haunted by the dead people.

You could tell that Johnny's dream was not their dream. They had questions as to how it would be built and where they could get the materials and the money.

The three older brothers—Johnny, Frank, and Marco—were always competing for leadership of the gang. Johnny and Frank were the strong-willed members of the gang, while Marco had a quiet way about him. He often didn't agree with them. Despite the fact that he was the smaller of the older brothers, he would stand up to them if he felt their positions were unfair or punitive.

Many times, each older brother put us in the position of choosing loyalty to one of them. When we chose positions not to our older brother's liking, we paid a price.

My brother Johnny often used the very effective tactic of a cold shoulder, not talking to me for days or not helping me with chores because he felt a sense of betrayal. We learned at an early age the price of loyalty versus righteous positions.

I could tell by the doubtful looks on the older brothers that they were not too keen on the idea of building a fort. The first concerns of all the gang were where would we get the materials to build it. They all thought the idea was a crazy, one that my brother probably conceived in one of his nightmarish schemes. Johnny did have a tendency with his vivid imagination to have nightmares.

And I think they were nervous about the location. It would be right at the edge of the old Protestant Cemetery. At our age, we were very superstitious. Often fascinated with the possibilities that the dead people could rise from their graves, push the gravestones away, and come over the fence. Listening to radio shows like *Inner Sanctum* fueled our fear of ghosts. We would sit transfixed staring at the radio as the announcer would always begin the show with creaking door background noise and introduce the next "haunter" of the show that night to scare the living daylights out of us.

After discussing the idea, we all thought that it was not practical to build a fort since we had no money nor materials to build it. Discouraged, we started to walk away with the intent of going back to the steps of the apartment building.

> But Johnny had a way to get under your skin and motivate you
> to anger or action. He would say something like this: "I thought
> you all had guts. I guess you're chickens and quitters," and then

*he'd imitate a chicken, putting all of us in the embarrassing posi-
tion of looking like cowards.*

The *chicken* word itself was lethal; it stopped our exodus. We all turned toward each other with a look that said, *I'm not a chicken.* The ultimate insult forced us to return.

Johnny had us gather around him. He knelt on one knee and drew the outline of the fort again in the dirt. With his hands over the outline, he followed the foundation of the fort, illustrating the placement and construction of the walls, entry, and exit points.

I remember him laying out the plan. "We can get the materials from scraps of wood lying around the neighborhood. We can do it. Just think, a fort only for us. It'll look like the one in the movie. We'll be free to do whatever we want. We can come and go as we please."

No one responded. He looked down at the drawing one more time. Getting up and dusting the dirt off his dungarees without saying anoth-er word, he pushed his way out of the circle. Johnny, sensing rejection, started walking home. He wasn't aware that our lack of a response meant that he had convinced us of the possibility of building a fort and the independence it would bring.

A hush came over the gang as each of us pondered his ideas.

With spontaneous smiles from all of us, we were sold on the idea. "Shit! It can work!"

Frank said, "I know where we can get the materials!"

We yelled out to Johnny to come back.

He returned to the gang with a triumphant look, like that of a base-ball player who had just hit a grand slam home run. His arms were outstretched pumping them up and down with the symbol of victory. I could feel his joy.

We were all smiling at one another when Johnny finally rejoined the circle. Some of the guys patted him on the back, anxious for his leadership on how to build the fort. I watched how everyone, who a few minutes before mocked him, now cheered him.

My brother stood his ground and rallied everyone. He grew several inches in my eyes that day and gave me one of my first lessons in perseverance.

When everyone settled down, Johnny asked Frank where we could get the materials.

Frank came up with the solution. We could get the materials from the old warehouses on Oakland Avenue. His idea of the old warehouses was ingenious and surprising, especially to Johnny and me. Since the old wooden warehouses were not far from our house just opposite the juvenile park on Oakland Avenue. Those abandoned warehouses were rotting and sinking into the swamp. They looked like a long row of garages. No one cared about them. Frank's idea was that we could take them apart piece by piece.

Johnny was concerned about the condition of the wood, whether it was rotted beyond use, because the warehouses were in the damp swamps. But many of us remembered that the upper clapboard was probably still useable.

We formed a circle again and knelt on the ground. Johnny picked up his stick again and, in earnest, did a detailed drawing of the fort with more detail on how we would get the materials. First, we would dismantle the good clapboard planks for our project. We would need enough material for a fort fifteen-by-fifteen feet. Ten feet from the outside perimeter of the walls, a two-by-one-foot moat would be dug and filled with dog dung, pointed sticks, and glass. The moat would be camouflaged with tree branches and with grass on top of those branches. The path from Purdy Street to the field and main door would be the only way any one of us could get in. If someone tried to sneak in any other way, they would fall into the moat and get dog dung on them or get scratched from the sticks and glass. Also, it would be the first line of defense in case we'd ever be attacked.

Then, pointing the stick to the fort outline, he drew a second line inside the square fort outline and broke off a portion of the stick placing it in the center. A catwalk three-feet wide would go around the entire square with two-by-three-foot ramps. The catwalk would need stronger planks than the clapboard from the old warehouse. He persuaded Marco and Michael, to 'borrow' the scaffold planks from their father's construction yard. The lookout platform would be four-by-four-feet square with cross braces into a pole to hold it. The pole for the lookout platform would come from a tree that we would chop down. The platform should be about fifteen-feet high and placed in the center of the fort with a wooden stepladder. The ladder for the platform would be wood rungs nailed to the post leading to the top of the platform. Three cutouts two-by-two-feet spaced three feet apart in the walls. Each cutout mounted with slingshots from the y-shaped ash tree branches. To access the slingshots at each cutout, a two-by-three-foot catwalk would be built. If enemies would ever attack us, we could jump up onto the catwalk and fire the slingshots. The straps for the slingshots can come from tire tubes that the Colonial Service station down the street throws away.

With a teasing smile, Johnny assigned Michael and me the task of getting the tire tubes. He figured that we wouldn't mind getting the tubes since we sometimes stopped to look at the pinup calendar in the back office on our way home from school.

Everyone roared while Michael and I blushed.

As we all studied his plans, Frank came up with another brilliant plan that would save us many hours of work. He suggested that we use the doors from the warehouses for the walls, figuring we needed about five for each side of the fort.

Marco was not convinced we could move doors. Carrying the doors, the distance from Oakland Avenue to Purdy Street would wear us down, and we would need three of us to carry one door. He thought it would be easier to carry the planks. But we were all keen on Frank's idea since it would save us time and the fort could be built sooner.

It looked like we were heading for another of their posturing when Michael came up with the idea of getting old carriages and using the wheels and axles to build a wagon, putting the axles on a two-by-four piece of wood and bracing the axles with bent-over nails. Then we'd place strips of clapboard for the floor bed to carry the lumber and the doors. The doors could be tied down on the wagon and moved with little effort on our part.

Johnny moved the conversation back to the carriages. "Ok, does anyone have any ideas on how we can get the carriages without getting in trouble?"

As he waited for our response, he tapped the stick, moving it up and down, right and left, over the fort outline he drew, much like a golfer before taking a swing at the ball. We were mesmerized with the stick movement. Instead of thinking about the carriages, the fort outline was growing deeper in our thoughts. Its possibilities were getting stronger.

We figured there was only one way we could get the carriages—from the Junk Man! He was a good person to know, especially if you had copper, aluminum, or zinc. After the war, in the late forties, junk metal and rags (because of their scarcity) were items that could be converted into cash. With the advent of the Korean War in 1950, the scarcity continued. My brother Johnny and I would scavenge the neighborhood for discarded metal and sell it to him. He gave us more money for pieces of metal than we could get from bottle deposit refunds. Scrounging for empty beer and soda bottles was dirty work. Every week, the Junk Man picked up stuff piled on the curbs in the neighborhood. If something was worth anything, people expected to get paid. If not, they left discarded junk there for him to pick up.

Our goal would be that on our way home from school, if we saw a pile of junk with an old baby carriage or anything else with four wheels, we'd take it since the neighbors were throwing it out anyway.

FOUR

"GO FIND THAT MUTT BEFORE HE GETS CAUGHT…..!"

We were familiar with the swamps and their treasures because of our dog Blackie. The swamp was a sanctuary for birds and other wildlife. It was a place that was completely hidden from the surrounding neighborhood. There we were able to act out our adventurous pursuits along with our dog Blackie.

Blackie was a mutt. He was part lab and part something else. He was totally black and had ears shaped like the head of a spear used by ancient Roman soldiers. He was a medium size dog. He had dark brown eyes with a penetrating stare. He always looked like he was weighing his next move. He had a tendency to bite people in the ass, so we had to try to intercept him whenever there were strangers passing through our back walkway or stopping to make a delivery.

Our home was located on the corner of Parsons Street and Oakland Avenue. Across the street was the office of Berlanti Construction Company. One time a man was going to those offices and used the sidewalk that cut through our property as a short cut. Blackie on hot summer days would lie under a concrete bench to stay cool. Next to the bench were steps leading to the end of the walkway. With the shade and his black color, you would never know he was there. When that man came to the steps and started to descend to the pavement below Blackie came out from under the bench and bit the man right in the ass, tearing his pants. Later that day the man knocked on our front door to tell my mom what happen. The conversation went like this.

"Mrs. Matero, I was passing through your backyard today and your dog bit me and tore my pants and now my suit is ruined. I think you should pay me for the damage done to it."

Mom answered with a smile, " I don't have to pay you a thing. You had no business passing through our back walkway. It is private property, and you passed at your own risk." She shut the door, and we never heard from him again.

The marshes and creek leading to the swamp pond were right across the street from our home. Today a portion of that marsh area and creek has been backfilled and covered with concrete and a commercial building.

My brothers and I learned to explore the marshes at an early age because of Blackie. He was an explorer. He would roam the swamp looking for prey. Sometimes when he came home, he was caked in the muck of the swamp. Other times he would stink of skunk cabbage. Many times, he would be missing for a day or more, and we would have to go out and search for him throughout the neighborhood. And when that happened, Mom would be infuriated.

"Go find that mutt before he gets caught by the Humane Society or killed by one of the animals!" Sonny would take Johnny and me, and we would fan out in the neighborhood or swamp looking for him.

The most challenging searches were when we had to look for him in the swamp. The thicket of willow trees, reeds and cattails was so dense that we could not see through them. The willow tree branches would overhang the creek. We had to push the reeds and cattails aside to follow the small path alongside the creek. We had to watch our footing. The willow tree branches made it difficult to see the edge of the path. Misjudging the edge would put you in the creek.

Amazingly that small path and the creek that ran beside it led us to a bigger pond, and from the pond to the larger creek, Beaver Swamp, that crosses the towns of Rye and Mamaroneck depositing in Long Island Sound.

It was always a beautiful experience going into the swamp, seeing the lush green willow trees with their branches and the reeds with their stately feather-like flower swaying in the wind. I would imagine ballerinas moving their arms. The cattails with their green leaves, guarding the swamp with their stiff straight stems and brown round flower beautiful to look at but with deceptively sharp leaves that often cut our hands as we pushed them aside opening to the pond.

When we went to search for our dog, yelling, "Blackie, come on Blackie," he would go deeper into the swamps to avoid us. Some of the times we caught him because his big pointed black ears moved and would stand out between the spaces of the reeds and cattails, and the three of us would corner him.

Eventually the swamps did Blackie in. He got very sick. Mom did everything she could to save him. She was about to give up on him. One day she was in the post office when the Postmaster of the Town, Mrs. Patterson noticed my mother's worried expression. She knew Mom's financial situation. When she found out about Blackie, she offered to pay for his care at the veterinarian. Through her kind generosity, Blackie's life got an extension of 6 months.

He loved the swamps. When my brothers and I buried him, we put him in a wooden fruit crate wrapped in a blanket and placed him besides the creek path that he loved, and we had a graveside ceremony bowing our heads in silent prayer. As we left, I looked back crying and murmuring his name, hoping somehow a miracle would happen. I hoped Blackie would come running out of the swamp muddy or smelling like a skunk so I could hold him again.

Blackie's roaming led us to the discovery of the swamp and marshes that we eventually shared with the gang and others in the neighborhood.

In the summer months, we'd raft in the creeks and pond or played war games. We discovered the old warehouses by accident when we were looking for wood for the rafts. The rafts we built were a mix of clapboard and logs held together with nails and rope. Often times I thought our rafts would sink as the water seeped through the spaces between the boards and log. The thrill of pushing them over the mirror-like water with the gentle wind carrying the sounds of birds and the beautiful orange golden fish in the water below made us felt a part of the swamp ecosystem.

We cleared the trails Blackie used to follow along the creek that led to the open area by the pond. Our biggest fear was to fall in the water or into the swamp mud. The swamp had a vibrant population of snapping turtles which bury themselves in the mud waiting for their prey. These turtles would snap at anything they found threatening, with a snap so powerful that it could easily shear fingers. We saw an example of that firsthand.

There was a family that lived on Park Avenue on a parcel opposite the swamp surrounded by reeds and cattails. There were no other houses to either side it. The only part of the house visible from the road was the front. We used to call the people that lived there the "Swamp People." One summer, the two brothers took a raft and paddled to the center of the pond to a cluster of lilies.

The six of us were at the solid bank edge of the pond bank watching them.

They were stationary, watching and waiting to see if a turtle was hunting for fish. When they saw some movement, they dove into the pond. The lilies rippled from the dive. It seemed like forever before they came up. I thought surely they were eaten up by the snapping turtles. Then they surfaced, smiling, holding two snapping turtles by their sides to prevent being bitten. The turtles must have weighed 30 pounds or more. We looked at one another, mouths opened, amazed that they were not hurt. Each of the turtles cocked its head to one side, waiting to bite. Showing off, the brothers took a stick and put it into the turtle's mouth. The stick snapped in pieces. All I could think of was that the brothers better get away before the turtle snaps at their fingers or toes. They put the turtles at the edge of the raft, pushed them off with another stick, and paddled back.

The lesson we learned was: Don't mess with the snapping turtles; otherwise, we could lose a hand or get a nasty bite someplace else. Each trek into the swamp, we were very careful where we stepped, not to disturb them in their nests.

The other object we had to avoid were the muskrat traps set by my brother Sonny and his friend Warren. My brother used to hunt for muskrat as a means of making some money to help Mom with her finances. Sonny and Warren, during the fall and winter months, would go into the swamp with muskrat traps and set them in different places in the swamp, following the trails left by the muskrat's tail. I watched them once opening the jaws of the trap and set the spring mechanism for the jaws to stay open. The trap was secured by chain with a ring at the end and a post driven through the ring into the ground.

As my brother was setting the trap, he turned to me. "Anthony, don't ever grab these open traps with your hand. They will break your fingers."

I asked to try one. As I opened the jaws, the tension was too great for me to hold on, and dropped it, my fingers barely escaping.

Sonny laughed. "Anthony, maybe when you get a little older you can help me."

Sonny and Warren would get up at five in the morning on school days to retrieve the traps. Sometimes I would get up early with them and enjoy the conversations they were having. Mom would make breakfast as she hummed and laughed, listening to the radio show *Klavan & Finch* playing music and humorous commentary on *WNEW 1130*, a staple in our home.

After breakfast they would go into the swamps and retrieve the musk-rats that were caught and died in the traps. When they came out of the swamp, my brother Sonny was carrying a few dead muskrats by their tails. I couldn't help but feel sorry for the muskrats. They were a loveable-looking animal with a face somewhat like a rat but more like a beaver. With their mixture of black and brown fur, I imagined them to be soft like a rabbit. Loveable as they looked, they could be quite nasty with their sharp claws and teeth. Sonny would carry them into the cellar of our house.

After school, Sonny and Warren would go to the cellar and skin the muskrats for their pelts. One day out of curiosity I went down to the cellar to see how they did it. It was awful.

They would string a grouping of muskrats pinching their hair and hang-ing them, their backs in a hump position. The light in the basement reflected off the animal's dormant eyes. They took the muskrats down, cleaned the fur, and meticulously skinned them by slicing into the rear so they could get under the skin, pulling the fur over the flesh. All that existed after that was a ball of flesh which they threw into a garbage pail and kept the prized fur pelt which needed to dry. Then they took the pelts and put them on twenty-one-inch wood stretchers, shaped like a skateboard, to dry. After the pelts dried, they put them in a carton and mailed them to Sears Roebuck, eventually collecting five dollars for each pelt.

It upset me that a muskrat, once a living creature, was cast aside into a garbage pail after its fur was collected. I went to my brother. "Sonny, I don't think I can ever do what you and Warren are doing to any animal. Both of you look like the ghouls in the movies. How can you do this?"

"Look, Anthony. I don't enjoy doing this. But you have to understand that our family needs the money. I have to help Mom out, otherwise she won't be able to make ends meet to keep us in the house. I hope you will never have to do anything like this."

With that, I understood. It was perhaps one of my first lessons in life: You have to do what is necessary to protect yourself and family. It was another part of Sonny's life dedicated to our family's survival. In the summer, he caddied at the golf course; in the winter, he trapped, leaving little time for himself to enjoy as a teenager, sacrificing his desire to play football and basketball with the high school teams.

Then there were other reasons to be careful in the swamp. There were snakes— black snakes and copperheads. We never knew where they were in the thicket of reeds and cattails. Occasionally we would see a black snake hanging from the tree. It was harmless unless you tempted it to bite you. The copperhead, on the other hand, was a different story. We feared a bite from any of them because it could be fatal.

By knowing and respecting the reptilian and muskrats swamp habitats, we were able to have adventures. Sometimes playing Marines, the rafts would be used as amphibious vehicles. We pushed them to the swamp bank, jumping off and charging the phantom enemy. We covered ourselves with reeds and willow tree branches, careful not to expose our position to the enemy, shifting our eyes right and left, waiting with our improvised wooden rifles for the enemy to attack. The only attack was from the mosquitoes who were having a feast. They bit me on my face and legs, and the itching became almost unbearable.

Tired of being Marines, it was time to be Tarzan. We would turn our attention to the willow trees that followed the swamp creek (Beaver Swamp Creek) all the way to Mamaroneck and dumped into Long Island Sound. Climbing the willow tree was the easy part. Grabbing the longest branch to swing from tree to tree was the hard part. The joy of yelling the Tarzan-cry of the jungle, grasping a branch of the next tree and then the next without falling into the water below gave us the feeling of invincibility. Our voices echoed across the swamp to the neighborhood streets, and the birds became alarmed and flew out of the marshes and trees.

In the winter months when the pond froze, it became an ice skating rink. The first time I tried on a pair of skates, my feet took to the ice and within one hour I was able to do a figure eight on the ice. I was a natural. The next use for the pond was to make it an ice hockey rink. We teamed up with other neighborhood boys and played the most brutal hockey games, using homemade hockey sticks crashing into legs and heads, miraculously with little damage. The net was a cluster of branches. The goalie's face protection was a beat-up , catcher's mask.

When the swamp creek froze in the winter it was an ice path that we could skate to Mamaroneck. Along the way, we met boys in other neighborhoods. When pausing for a rest, two boys, Steve and Lester, became very friendly with us. Their street, Wendall Lane, dead-ended at the creek. When they saw us and struck up a conversation, the bond formed.

The best part one winter was when the pond froze, the ice thick to the muck below. On one of the coldest nights, the older brothers Sonny, Jerry, Warren, and their friends Tom, Dominic, and Vinney, brought piles of wood and placed them in the center of the pond. A bonfire was lit at night. The flames reached ten foot or more, radiating heat around the pond area. We skated with the warmth of an indoor rink. The fire shadows were reflecting like dancing fingers off the willow trees and reeds. When the flame died down, it was time to go home.

And when we did get home, Mom would be sitting in the kitchen waiting for us. From our house, she could see the flames reaching up. "*Il tuo pazzo,* what's wrong with you boys? I could see the fire from here. Sonny, you should know better! I don't want to see you do that again! *Capisci?*" End of conversation. No excuses. When Mom was like this, it was best you say nothing. When I went to bed that night of the bonfire, I could still feel the warm glow of the fire and feel the excitement, laughter, and closeness with all the boys.

We rarely ventured into the swamps without another person. It was just too risky. A reptile could bite, or you could slip and fall in the creek. If you had nothing to grab onto, you could sink in the muck or there could be some unsavory characters in them.

One time my brother Johnny came home and told us the what happened when he was walking along Oakland Avenue. Four boys from another neighborhood came out of the swamps by Haviland Street carrying bows and arrows. They knew my brother was the leader of the Purdy Street Gang. They were bigger than Johnny. They corralled him, tied his hands behind his back, and dragged him to a big oak tree at the end of Haviland Street. Johnny told us, once they tied him up, they stepped back and started to shoot arrows at him. Thankfully most missed. But some did not. Those that did, hit the legs and chest stinging him. A man who was walking by saw what the boys were doing and yelled at them, chasing them away, and he came over to Johnny and untied him. Johnny was a wreck when he came home. He never knew who those boys were or where they came from. He always thought they might have come from the next town over—Rye, NY.

That incident dwelled in him for the longest time. One day he made up his mind that it was the boys that lived in Rye on Coolidge and Harding Avenue. He said to me that day, "Anthony, get a long stick. I'll see if Marco and Michael want to come. But we are going after those boys in Rye and scare the hell out of them for what they did to me!"

The four of us went into the neighborhoods, riding our bikes and using the sticks as spears like Indians on the warpath. The Rye boys, seeing us charge at them, scattered like ants.

Johnny yelled, "You better not come into our territory again or we'll beat you up."

It may have worked because, after that, we didn't see too many kids on the opposite sides of the swamp creek bordering Rye.

> I think back to Blackie and how he opened up our world. How interested would we have been in the swamp if we did not have to look for him? The swamp was another world. Our neighborhood that stretched from Parsons Street to Halstead Avenue School was about a square mile. The swamp was more than that. It was creeks and ponds and hidden wildlife, the jungle of Tarzan, the adventures of sailors, and the heroics of Marines. What a time.

FIVE

"FONGOOL TO YOU, OLD WITCH!"

One afternoon on our way home from school, I spotted two oversized carriages next to a junk pile on the curb in front of a neighbor's house. They were exactly what we needed. The spokes in the wheels looked strong and the rubber on the tires hardly worn. The axles were strong enough to handle the weight of a door. Johnny and I figured that the junk man had already passed through the neighborhood and probably decided not to take them, so we took them home. We decided that the wagons would be best built behind the pigeon coop in our backyard. It was wide enough to conceal what we were doing, and concealment was paramount.

The following weekend, the gang met at our house. It was a warm sunny day that last weekend in May. We were anticipating the end of the school year in a few short weeks. Our short sleeves rolled up, much like the Italian construction workmen did when they dug ditches or worked with stone. Michael brought the plans for the wagons drawn on a brown Kraft paper lunch bag. *It was pretty farsighted for him to do it that way. The paper was strong enough to withstand our constant handling of the plans.*

We dismantled the carriages, taking the steel axle and wheels. We took two four-by-eight-foot scaffold planks and joined them together with two-by-four wood strips. Then we attached the axles to blocks from two-by-fours to the front and back ends, securing them with 5D nails bent to hold the axles in place. The pigeons in the coop, disturbed by our movements with the planks and banging of nails, cooed louder, fluttered their wings, and moved from their perches to the floor, gathering by the main door, and paced back and forth looking to leave the coop. They feared something was about to happen to them.

My brother Johnny got distracted and became irritable with their cooing and directed me to let them out of the coop. He figured they would calm down and be out of the way if they were out of the coop and flying. Most times the pigeons would come right back to the coop after their flights. But with all the activity they would stay away free to perch on anyone's roof. The old lady who lived across the street from us did not like our pigeons or us. She hated the pigeons for the dung they left behind. And she hated us because we were always playing outside, making noise children make when they play. In a way, I thought she had a point about the pigeon dung. I was the designated cleaner of the coop. At least once a week I had to scrape the floor and perches and dump it into the garbage. It was no easy job since the dung stuck to the wood like glue and stank. I would clean it sometimes with one hand holding my nose, especially on hot days. Once the pigeon dung dried up on the old lady's roof, it had white spots. Only a driving rain would clean it off.

Johnny figured it would be close to 7:00 p.m. before our pigeons returned. The old lady wouldn't know they were on her roof because it would be getting dark and she went to bed early. He loved taking chances.

I went to the front of the coop. The pigeons were on their perches, cooing louder anticipating their release. I opened the latch on the loft doors and the pigeons flew upward in a sudden flurry, catching the air currents to go higher and higher. Each circled the house. The leader kept the circle intact, assembling the entire flock. They looked like a formation of planes moving eastward, taking them as far away as the next two towns. What a sight! A flight to freedom. I could feel a smile on my face. I gazed at their wings fluttering in the breeze, thinking of the places I could visit if I could fly like them.

In our minds, the wretched and nosey old lady was a witch. I remember her as always peeping out the window from behind curtains, observing the neighbors. She was a gossiper and created rumors about anyone she did not like. With bulging eyes, she looked very much like the Wicked Witch of the West in *The Wizard of Oz* movie. The only difference between them was facial color. The Wicked Witch of the West had a green face; our neighbor's face had an orange tint like a pumpkin. She complained to other parents that Johnny and I made too much noise when we played. She was always accusing us of stealing if something in the neighborhood was missing, calling the police and make our lives downright miserable.

There was a pathway between Parsons and Soulard Streets. Johnny and I used it as a shortcut to meet Michael and Marco when going to school in the morning and to meet them to hang around the neighborhood. The old lady's house bordered that path. She would throw garbage at us from her third-floor apartment when she heard Johnny and I talking on our way to school. One time, as we were walking through the path to meet Marco and Michael I heard her window open. I glanced up and saw her tilt a pot. Streaming out of it was a dark brown liquid trail. In that moment I gasped, thinking she was pouring diarrhea on us. I yelled to Johnny who was a couple steps behind me, "Johnny, watch out. The witch is pouring crap out the window."

Johnny could not get out of the way. A steam of cold lentil soup landed on my brother's head. I watched helplessly as it descended on his head and clothes. The lentils descended like rain drops, some getting into his hair others down the back of his neck and sticking to his shirt.

"Crap!" he said. "*Fongool* to you, old witch!" He reinforced the words with an upward obscene gesture of the finger and arm; then he raced home to change.

When he got home, he said, "Mom, look at what that old lady across the street did! She threw cold lentil soup out of her window at us when we were walking on the path. I have slimy lentil in my hair and on my clothes."

Mom had been in the kitchen cleaning up the breakfast dishes. She looked in disgust at the mess on his clothes, holding her hands to her lips, quivering with anger as she slammed the dish towel down on the table. "If that women ever bothers you again, I will have her arrested!"

> *Mom had good reason to say that. The old lady was always spreading rumors about my widowed mother, some worse than others. One night, my mother had caught her crouched below her bedroom window. The old lady started a rumor that my mom was seeing male friends. She was spying for that very reason to shore up her rumor. Infuriated, Mom had chased after her. "If I ever see you on my property again, I'll call the police." The threat was enough to keep the old lady away from us for a while—until the lentil incident. She was a vindictive person.*

The screech of the rusted clothesline pulley brought me back from daydreaming. Johnny and I looked at one another. It was a familiar sound. Mom was pushing the clothesline while hanging laundry. Johnny put up his hand stopping the gangs hammering and pointing his finger toward Mom. We all looked at one another, and then panic came over us as we rustled the materials, hiding them under the pigeon coop. We knew Mom would see us in a few minutes as she pushed the line toward the coop.

Johnny's face had worry written all over it, forewarning the gang not to say anything to our mom if she came to see what we were doing.

The clothes came nearer. With each push Mom made hanging a garment, the line came closer to the pole behind the coop. She had hanging clothes down to a science. She would hold a garment up to the line clamp one wooden clothespin on it while holding another clothes pin in her mouth. Each garment would go on the line faster than the previous one with her system. It was always an amazing ritual. Shirts, pant legs, and undergarments performed a colorful dance in the wind. It was like watching a gathering of invisible people.

The screeching pulley finally stopped at the pole; the line was full. Mom gazed in our direction with her hands on her hips and a look of *What are they up to?*

She finally stepped forward and started walking toward us. Mom always walked fast, but this time she walked faster than usual. Meanwhile, Johnny was thinking up answers.

When Mom arrived, she stopped and surveyed the area. It was almost like we could see her thoughts: *What are they doing with all this junk?*

We all looked at one another.

"Anthony, Johnny," she said. "What are you building?"

Her unexpected appearance created anxious looks on everyone. They did not want her to go back to their parents and tell them what we were doing. The gang walked away, scattering like ants, leaving Johnny and I alone with Mom. Their sudden abandonment only aroused her curiosity more.

Anticipating another question, Johnny said, "We're building carts. We're gonna use them for racing on Soulard Street." Any mention of us playing in the street sent shivers up her spine because of the car accident I was in when I was six years old.

"Johnny, is this your idea? *Tu sei pazzo!* Your brother almost got killed by a car, and now you want all the neighborhood boys to get killed."

In his crafty way, my brother answered, "Ah, Mom. No cars go down Soulard Street. We'll be okay."

Mom said, "No. No. Stop now and throw this junk away."

Then Johnny leveled with her. "OK, Mom. Look, we're gonna build the carts to haul lumber from the swamp buildings."

Mom stared at him. She always suspected Johnny had something up his sleeve since the funeral procession of cars line up outside our house when Johnny snuck out and let the air out of everyone's tires.

"Vieni qui! Lumber for what?" Mom asked, motioning for him to come to her.

He was biting his lip, a sign he was thinking of what to say. He dropped the hammer and held Mom's hands with both of his hands. He always had a charming way with her. "Mom, we didn't want you to worry. We're not gonna build racing carts. But we're gonna use the lumber to build a place to hang out when we play on Purdy Street. We need the carts to carry the lumber. It's gonna be our clubhouse. All we're gonna do is hang around in it once in a while. We are building a hut a little bigger than this pigeon coop."

 Our pigeon coop was about eight feet by eight feet; the fort was going to about two times that size. His description of the hangout to Mom was far different than the one he envisioned.

Trying hard not to laugh, Mom said, "Johnny, you are going to drag wood from the swamps to Purdy Street to build a clubhouse? You're all crazy. And you know I don't want you near the swamps."

"Ah, Mom, it's only for a while. We just need to get some of the materials from the old warehouses to use for building our fort. Most we will be there is a couple of days once the carts are built."

"Ok. But only for a couple of days. Hurry up and finish what you're doing. It's almost supper time."

She walked away chuckling and shaking her head, convinced that it was a foolish project. I wondered why she didn't question Johnny more.

SIX

"TO THE BEACH!"

Finally, it was June, and the school year ended. Classes were released almost simultaneously at 3:00 p.m., resulting in a stampede as students raced together through the halls, screaming with joy, "Free at last! No more pencils, no more books, no more teachers' dirty looks!" They'd push the two huge double front doors open, and ran down the steps to the sidewalk on Halstead Avenue, scattering like a flock of birds going in different directions.

We ran by the monument of Christopher Columbus, a white marble statue that stood on a pedestal in front of the Halstead Avenue school facing Halstead Avenue and Broadway. His right arm and index finger pointed forward, symbolizing the discovery of America. Each day that I passed that statue, I wondered how he could travel the seas in the clothes he wore: a heavy draping robe that looked like a winter coat with a fur lining, a skirt, and stockings that only went up to his knees! But we all looked up to him. Passing the statue, we would imitate its pose, lifting our arms and pointing our index fingers, and shouting together in adoration and pride, "Christopher Columbus! Our adventurer!"

The freedom and anticipation of summer pleasures rose within us with each step on our way home, our jubilant voices echoing ever so loudly that not even the traffic on Halstead Avenue was able to drown them out. We were putting the adult world on notice that the young-of-heart were about to begin their summer adventures. Storekeepers stood in their doorways smiling. Maybe they were reminiscing about their youth. They were enjoying watching us chattering and playing on our way to summer's freedom.

The first days of that July, we began the work on the fort. First, we concentrated on the thicket of woods in the back corner of the lot on Purdy Street. With axes, shovels, and picks, we began clearing the brush and small trees. We underestimated the physical effort. The work was harder than we had anticipated. Our exuberance for building the fort was diminishing.

Our thirst so great that, in the first two hours of working, the water in our coke bottles was consumed. Combined with the heat, our stamina weakened. The older brothers decided that we needed to stop for a while and rest up. We sat around in a circle like workmen at construction sites enjoying a restful pause, some of us picked up small pebbles and randomly threw them into the center of the circle. Since we were out of water, I took the empty coke bottles home and filled them.

On my way back, I saw Michael leaving the cave on Purdy Street which was about twenty-five yards from where the fort was going to be built. We used the cave to store all the tools and cigarettes while building the fort. None of us knew where Michael hid them except my brother Johnny. He wanted to make sure that no one else would take them when we were not around. He was waving a pack of *Parliament* cigarettes in his hand signaling to me it was time to "light up."

We returned to our worksite with the cigarettes and water. Johnny handed one cigarette out to each of us. None of us knew how to inhale. We just puffed away as we sat in a circle, blowing smoke rings like the big *Camel* advertisement in Times Square or plumes of smoke like Native Americans warning smoke signals

Suddenly, we all heard a sound coming from behind the shrubbery. Someone was spying on us.

Scattering, we dug a small hole and buried our cigarettes. Too late. Out of nowhere, our two older brothers, Jerry and Sonny, who were sixteen, emerged. Sonny and Jerry often acted like they were our protectors. Many times, they would try to stop us in our adventurous pursuits. We were always able to evade them by agreeing at first, only to continue with our plans when they were out of sight.

We took quick glances at one another, wondering which one of us was going to tell them what we were up to. Finally, we all turned toward Johnny. He took the cue. He had to come up with some explanation. He was nervous. I could tell by the way he sometimes would grab the corner of his front pants pocket and loop his thumb inside and rub the rest of his hand on the outside.

Sonny knew this as well and, often times, would bear down on him through sheer intimidation to get what he wanted out of Johnny—the truth. But that tactic always had the opposite effect.

Johnny had a gift of keeping stories straight. Knowing that the week before he told our mother of our plans for the clubhouse and wagons, he probably thought that Mom sent Sonny to check up on us. He proceeded to tell him the same story.

Sonny and Jerry huddled, whispering between them. You could see a smile of satisfaction. They heard what they wanted. He came and stood over us.

Sonny was overpowering in height. He was about six foot one. The tallest of us, Frank was six inches shorter to him. And we were all smaller than Frank. The guys knew how forceful Sonny could be.

He lectured us not to use the club house for anything bad. Then he warned Johnny and I that, if anything bad did happen, he would whack us good. Jerry was mainly looking at his brothers, Marco and Michael, warning them not take anything from their father's business to build the fort, because if their father found out, they would get more than a pat on the butt. And he cautioned his brothers not to take any of their father's cigarettes either. Our parents saw Sonny and Jerry as an extension of their eyes and ears, expecting them to discourage us from mischievous behavior and reporting back to them.

Crap, we thought, they knew we were smoking.

Then they demanded to know where we hid the cigarettes, since they smelled the smoke when they arrived. And if we didn't hand them over, they would tell our parents.

Jerry and Sonny, although sixteen, also did not have permission to smoke. Jerry was signaling that he had no qualms about his brothers taking the cigarettes, as long as he could get some from them. So, we reached a comprise with them. When we had cigarettes and if they needed them, they could meet us at the fort, and we would give them what cigarettes we had. As long as they did not tell on us, we would not tell on them.

At least once a week while we were building the fort, Sonny and Jerry would check on us and ask for cigarettes. While there, they were critical about our plans to build the fort. They thought we would never be able to build it. And if we did build it, the walls would probably collapse. We didn't take their criticism seriously. In the end, we got the last laugh. Sonny and Jerry, with their friends Tommy, Vinney, and Dominic, started a project in the late spring to build a boat that could be used in the marshes. In order for them to work on it without weather interference, they built the boat in Jerry's basement. They finished it in June, just before we started clearing the lot in July. When they went to take the boat out of the basement, they realized that the basement doorway was not wide enough. They had to dismantle a portion of the hull to get it out. Once they got it out of the basement they had to re-build the hull. When they finished, they announced to other boys in the neighborhood that they were going to launch the boat. Everyone was excited watching the five of them carry the boat and how excited they were as they anticipated floating it in the marsh creeks. It made me feel really good knowing that, if you put your mind to something, anything is possible. When they got to the creek and put the boat in the water, it listed to the right and almost sank. We all laughed. If anyone would get into the boat, it would have capsized.

The disappointment and embarrassment on their faces was heartbreaking. My brother Sonny was so angry, that he threw one of the wood braces across the marshes and scared a duck into flight. They realized now that, when they took the boat apart, it upset the precision measurements of the hull. A few days later, the five of them came up with an idea to put two empty fifty-five-gallon drums on each side of the boat to prevent it from listing. It looked more like a pontoon boat with pontoons above the draft line as opposed to below it.

After Sonny and Jerry left, we continued to clear the lot, but the heat from the sun weakened us. Beads of sweat were pouring off us. Our fingers were cut from pulling the bushes and roots of the trees. Blisters formed in the center of our hands. Finally, after five hours, we quit, and plopped down on the ground exhausted.

About five days later, the lot up to the fence around the old Protestant cemetery was cleared and ready for the next stage.

The next week, we dug out the moat that would stretch five feet be-yond the front walls of the fort. The dirt caked our hands and faces. Our skin was burnt orange-red from the sun on the fairest of us—not an issue for Johnny and Marco who had darker complexions. Our crew stripped t-shirts and dungarees were dirt brown. Tempers were short, worn out by the backbreaking work of clearing the land and digging the moat.

It didn't take long for us to slow down. Everyone was getting frustrated with the physical effort and time. We would talk less about the fort and more about playing ball, going to the beach, or just riding our bikes in the neighborhood. Interest in the fort was losing its importance. Coming to the lot to work every day was turning us off. The gang was pretty dispirited. Arguments broke out. Some of us believed that we should keep going and not let up because we were making progress. Others just wanted out—period. They did not like working in the humidity. The last thing they wanted to do all summer was to be dirty and sweaty. The decision could go either way. But none of us wanted to ruin everything that we worked for. As friends do when they work out their differences, we decided to work on the fort some days and, on other days, to play ball, or go to Oakland Beach and the Playland Amusement Park in Rye. It was the best thing we did to keep the gang together.

Dropping our tools, we shouted, "To the beach!" All of us jumped on our bikes to head home as fast as we could—before we'd change our minds. We put on our bathing suits and jumped on our bikes again.

> I remember peddling my bike down Purdy Street like a motorcycle cop in pursuit of a speeding car. The wind felt good , as it flowed through my hair and brushed against my face.. Following right behind me was my brother, Johnny.

We all met at the corner of Oakland Avenue and Park Avenue for the three-mile bike ride to Oakland beach. The gang lined up like a motorcycle club, one behind the other. Johnny took the lead, Frank and Marco the rear. Park Avenue intersected with Route One, also known as the Boston Post Road, a heavily traveled commercial truck route.

When we arrived at intersection, the sounds from the cars and trucks were frightening. The rumble of the heavy trucks bearing down on one another, moving like the boxcars of a freight train. The roaring motors were so deafening that we could barely hear each other. The black smoke from their engines, billowing from their exhaust pipes, laid heavily over the humid air of that summer day.

Johnny cautiously approached the crossing, and called out to Frank to check the rear to make sure everyone was lined up. He turned to us and waved his arm in a forward motion, signaling us to cross. We had very little time. With a small opening between trucks, we raced across, pushing our bikes to avoid the oncoming trucks, hoping to get to the safety of the sidewalk. Closer they came, honking their horns in panicked rhythm and flashing their lights, warning us. With each horn blast, my hair curled up the back of my neck as I imagined a stampede of elephants about to crush us.

One by one, we reached the safety of the sidewalk.

As a couple of the drivers passed, they tapped their heads and yelled out, "You crazy kids could have been killed!"

My brother Johnny smiled and gave them a mocking wave and *thank you* bow. God only knows how much this angered the drivers.

As we had reached safety, we paused, dropped our bikes on the sidewalk, and sat down at the edge of the grass boundary forming the perimeter of Rye Wood Country Club, watching the golfers with their caddies. I was fascinated by the players and how they addressed the ball, moving the club in short left to right motions before taking one full swing at it. I was perplexed by why it took so long for them to swing.

I wondered what it was like to be rich and belong to exclusive clubs like that and play a game of golf anytime you wanted to. I also thought of my brother Sonny who probably was caddying to make some money for our family, while we were out playing our games, and I wondered what he was thinking carrying the heavy golf bags while we played. He would come home after caddying during the summer months, shirt sweaty from the long hot days carrying two bags just to make ten dollars a weekend. He would leave the house on a Saturday and Sunday morning at six in the morning and not come home until six at night. No wonder he came home so late, given how long it took a player to swing at the ball! He would only keep two dollars of his earnings and hand the rest over to Mom to make ends meet. He really never enjoyed summers the way we did since he was the oldest and had to help with the family finances. His help often gave Mom enough to help buy the essentials, food and clothes. The social security check never covered all of her expenses.

SEVEN

"DON'T SAY ANYTHING TO ANYBODY. DO YOU UNDERSTAND?"

Rested, we picked up our bikes and continued to Oakland Avenue where the bike ride was remarkably enjoyable despite the fact that the road had no sidewalks. For one mile, we rode our bikes down an incline with arms spread like eagles. Letting my towel blow in the wind, I imagined myself as a bird, or as a World War I fighter pilot with me mimicking the rat-a-tat-tatting of a machine gun.

Oakland Avenue dead-ended at a low wrought iron fence atop a high wall that separated the neighborhood from Oakland Beach. From the top of that wall to the beach below, it was a steep drop to the sand. To the right of the fence was a rocky hill covered with bushes and small trees. It, too, was cordoned off. The purpose of the fence was preventative, meant to stop anyone from falling onto the sand far below or sneaking into the private beach through the wooded area.

Since we had no money, our only option was to sneak in.

Arriving at the beach, we parked our bikes in the bike stand by the main entrance. Then we went back to the low wrought iron fence. Obstacles meant opportunity for us. One by one, we squeezed through the wrought iron bars and gingerly moved from bar to bar sideways to the path in the wooded area. It took some guts to do this. With each step, we made sure our footing was firm. A slip up could send one of us crashing to the bottom and, if lucky, landing in the sand instead of hitting the stone wall. Miraculously, no one had a misstep.

Once one of us arrived at the edge of the wooded area bordering the beach sand, that person became the lookout for the next guy, making sure none of the lifeguards spotted us. If they did, we'd be escorted out the main gate.

One by one, we assembled on the beach. Laying our towels on the sand and disrobing, we ran and dove into the refreshing waters of Long Island Sound. Six of us diving in at one time caused an eruption of water shooting geysers upward. It was exhilarating to feel the cool water after sweating from building the fort and riding our bikes for almost four miles.

Swimming for two hours was sufficient to cool us off. It was about 3:30 p.m. when we decided on our next adventure.

Next to Oakland Beach is Rye Beach, an area reserved for Rye residents only. The two beaches were separated by a chain link fence and an eddy leading into the water. Spanning Rye Beach was a raised boardwalk shaped like a crescent moon that stretched the entire two-and-a-half mile length of the beach and ended at the speedboat dock and former ferry dock. About three quarters of the way, the boardwalk lined up with Playland Amusement Park.

We were all lying down on our towels, eyes on the clouds and watching gulls flying. Johnny, Marco, and Frank turned over and laid face-down on their towels. They were talking among themselves and staring like dogs in heat at two older girls behind us who were lying down on their towels facing us, with their suit straps loosened. They were trying to plan on how to approach the girls but decided not to because they feared the girls would either laugh at them or slap them.

As we all lay there on the sand, the sounds of the boardwalk and the aroma of food from the concession stands turned our interest away from the beach to a discussion about the boardwalk and amusement park rides. We all wanted to go on the rides, but there was one problem: We had very little money among us. Though we knew from overhearing the older brothers, Sonny and Jerry, say that when they were our age, they got money by going under the boardwalk and sifting through the sand for coins to buy tickets for the rides in the amusement park.

We decided to fan out. Some of us would crawl under the boardwalk by the concession stands. The rest would search under the main boardwalk leading to the pier. We were hoping that some bathers or amusement park patrons, after purchasing a refreshment, dropped their change and it fell through the crevices between each plank to the sand below.

Everyone agreed to the plan. The other challenge was that, in order to get under the boardwalk, we had to get into Rye Beach. Since we were not Rye residents, going through the main entranceway was not an option.

We tossed our towels, t-shirts, dungarees and sneakers over the chain link fence onto Rye Beach, making sure the lifeguards at each beach didn't see us. Then we swam beyond the point of the chain link fence and rocky jetty separating the two beaches.

In the water, we mimicked Navy frogmen slowly paddling arms in a butterfly stroke motion until we were beyond the jetty formation. Rounding the jetty, slowly swimming toward Rye Beach, our heads bobbed up and down to avoid detection by the lifeguard on Rye Beach. Where other children were frolicking in the water and sand, we sat with them in the water or sand, concealing that we were uninvited guests.

Once out of the water, we assembled on the beach and retrieved the towels. Some of us moved to the portion of the boardwalk where the food and novelty concessions were, and the others went under the main boardwalk. We sifted the sand carefully like miners searching for gold, stopping after each sift, letting the sand slip through our fingers, hoping to catch a coin so we could get the tickets for the one ride we wanted to experience at the Playland Amusement Park—The Dragon Coaster.

The gang loved roller coasters. So much so that the summer before this they undertook a major project to create a roller coaster that would give them the exhilaration of a real one. Taking two twenty-foot wooden ladders, courtesy of Mr. Bisceglia's junk pile, and joining them with wood braces nailed to each side and ropes tied to the bottom and top rung of each ladder. There was a huge hole across the street from our house, bordering the path by the old lady's house that we walked on every day and the apartment building about a half a block away and at the back of Mr. Bisceglia's construction yard. The hole was created by landscapers taking soil from the lot. Over time, it had become overgrown. The gang carved a path the width of the ladders, placed them in a 45 degree position to the bottom. We got boxes from the First National Store garbage heap. They would be used as our roller coaster cars. We placed them at the top of the hole and rode straight to the bottom of the hole, steering it from going off the ladder by righting it each time it started to veer off, by pushing it with a stick away from the edge. At the end of the ride, the box hit the ground so hard we were catapulted out. The old lady across the street from us went nuts with all the noise we made. Leaning out of her window and banging a pot to get our attention, she yelled, "Go home, or I'll call the police!"

We counted the change when everyone returned from sifting the sand. If we collected more than two dollars, it would be enough for a couple of rides, but not enough for admission to the Dragon Coaster. The gang was really upset that we could not go on that ride.

But my brother, Johnny, let the gang know that all was not lost. He had an idea. Our Aunt Josephine's cousin worked at the ticket booth by the Dragon and Airplane coasters. We knew her as "Rose S," and she knew Johnny and me. "Maybe we can get a book of tickets for nothing."

Marco was skeptical on how someone could give us free tickets for nothing without getting into trouble. He just gave Johnny an exasperated, disbelieving look, rolling his eyes and turning his head from left to right.

Johnny insisted that we try. He had good reason to try because Aunt Josephine was adamant that *Rose S.* told her that, if anyone in the family needed tickets, it was ok to ask. The other concern for some of the gang was that, if she did give us the tickets she might get in trouble.

We put on our dungarees and t-shirts, then started toward the boardwalk where we put on our Keds sneakers for the walk to Playland.

As we walked the boardwalk from the beach area, the crowds became more dense. We were like Snow White's dwarves compared to the size of the walkers. We looked to the right to make sure we were heading toward the main entrance of the park. As we neared it, band music was bellowing from speakers.

At the main entrance, we could go in one of two directions. The walkways branched left or right. Each side had rides, and we could hear the joyful screams of people on them. The asphalt walkways were separated by a huge lawn with a brilliant array of flowers. It was magic. Thousands of people were happily enjoying the festive feeling of the park, eating cotton candy, hot dogs, pizza, ice cream, or drinking soda.

Not one parent was scolding their children about what to eat. It was heaven. The sound of the music, the array of colors, and the joyful screams encouraged us to move faster toward the rides.

One of the rides was the Grand Carousel. We were mesmerized by it. The life size horses lined up in rows of three, frozen in position of racing, sixty-six horses in all. Each horse was carved from wood, their skin painted a glossy brown, white, black, and yellow. Their saddles and wraps were painted and decorated with a kaleidoscope of mixed brilliant colors. Their manes were sculptured to appear as if flowing in the wind.

We were fascinated with the movement of these carved horses. Starting off slowly at first, the life-sized horses gently moved up and down on the rod, and the riders were smiling and yelling, "Yippee ki yay!" while pulling the harness and waving their arms until the carrousel increased its speed. A frightening, thunderous noise arose from the motors that increased the motion of the horses going up and down; it sounded like a stampede. They were spinning so fast that the riders held on to the horse saddle for dear life.

Then we came to the kind of rides that caused the most fear in me. The Airplane Coaster and the Dragon Coaster, both of them screeching downward, the wooden cross-beamed structure shifting as the coasters catapulted down each hill. Riders were screaming, some with fear but others with joy. I gawked with my mouth open, thinking surely the ride was going to collapse.

We finally came to the ticket booth where *Rose S.* worked. The booth was just large enough for one person. She was busily handing out tickets, looking up only to see the length of the waiting line. When she saw us, her discomfort became apparent. Her eyes which normally had a bulge, seemed to bulge more with a surprised *Oh, shit* look on her face.

It was clear the only way we were going to get her to talk to us was to stand in line until we got to the window. Once there, my brother Johnny whispered, not wanting others in the line to hear him. "Hi, *Rose S.* Aunt Josephine said we could get some tickets for the rides."

Some of the people in the line behind craned their necks toward the front, trying to determine how long it would take and why the kid up front was so quiet. They could see he wasn't reaching into his pockets for money.

Rose was quick to respond. "Johnny, shh! Come to the back of the booth."

Johnny went behind the booth. She opened the door, looking right, then left, making sure no one was watching.

"Johnny, here's a couple of books for you and the boys." She threw two books in a gentle arc for him to catch. "Don't say anything to anybody. Do you understand?" And with a have-a-good-time smile, waved us off.

Having caught the books, Johnny signaled for us to follow him.

People in line were surely wondering what just happened. More than likely, I think *Rose S.* wouldn't jeopardize her job to give us the books for nothing. She probably had a discount with the park and bought the tickets with her own money.

Johnny figured we had enough tickets for all of us to get on the Dragon Coaster. The mere mention of that coaster and the earlier images of seeing the wood crossbeams shift made my stomach turn. Everyone else jumped with glee. They couldn't get on the ride fast enough, running all the way to the entrance gate of the coaster. Everybody, that is, except me. With my eyes and head cast down, I reluctantly walked toward the gate.

The gang could see I was scared. They called me out, "Are you coming, Anthony? What's the matter? Are you a chicken?"

Well, if there was one word I hated and still hate, it's *chicken*. I always thought it was a bully word. And I was determined not to be bullied. I lifted my head, quickened my pace, and ran toward them, ready to launch myself into the first one in my path.

"Whoa, Anthony! Cool down. We're only busting your chops," Michael said, trying to calm the confrontation.

He stopped me just in time.

Johnny could see I was really upset and that maybe I didn't want to go on the Dragon Coaster. "Look, Anthony, if you don't wanna go on the coaster, that's okay. You can wait here at the gate for us until we finish our ride."

All I heard was, *Look, Anthony, we understand that you're a chicken.*

"No, I'll go. Nobody's gonna call me a chicken."

We lined up at the gate and were eventually put into cars. Sitting next to me was Michael. The attendant came by each car and pulled down the safety bar, locking us in place. When he did that, a sense of finality came over me. I realized at that point there was no way to get out of this unless I screamed to the attendant to get me out. I would not do that. I was a captive to my commitment.

The warning bell clanged, indicating the ride was about to start and alerting everyone to hold onto their safety bars. Slowly the cars moved up and out from under the starting point and onto the incline. All I could see were the tracks and railings reaching up into the blue sky.

Fear was building inside me. My eyes squeezed tightly shut, and my heart was beating so fast it felt like it was about to come out my mouth. My knuckles were turning white from gripping the safety bar. Finally reaching the crest, the coaster slowly accelerated down the first series of peaks and valleys and leveled off at other points, only to repeat. I opened my eyes and turned to Michael, shouting over the noise of the car wheels clattering on the tracks. "This isn't so bad!" I yelled with a smile.

The tracks suddenly made a severe drop of forty-five degrees, propelling us downward, jerking us, causing my chest to press against the safety bar. Then the ride accelerated upward to the highest point of the coaster, slowly leveling off, giving us a panoramic view of the park and Long Island Sound. I thought that this was what a bird must see as it hovers.

But the wonderment was short-lived. Suddenly the car jerked right, then left, the tracks disappeared and gave me the feeling that the cars would launch into mid-air. Then the car made a sudden drop, at speed greater than any other point in the ride, casting us forward, pressing my chest against the safety bar again. The tracks leveled for a short distance, but the cars were still moving at breakneck speed, and we were suddenly launched upward, faster and faster, up and then down, twisting and turning, as the cars followed the tracks.

I became tense at each twist and turn, and I could see Michael laughing. At several points, I thought surely both of us were going to be thrown out of the car. Michael was pressing so hard against me that I was hanging over the side of the car. With his strong arms, he tried to lean to his side of the car and at the same time pull me away from the edge. But the centrifugal force was so great that he was not able to reposition himself. As this was happening, the wood beams of the coaster structure came so close that I thought surely I wouldn't get to the ground safely and live to see another day.

The coaster leveled off and made a series of short drops, temporarily calming me. Then, without warning, the twists and turns started again, and we were accelerated upward. Up we went, faster and faster. If there had been a picture taken on that day, it would show me with my eyes closed, praying. All I wanted to do as we kept going up again was to get the hell off that coaster.

Then we dropped gently, though the speed was increasing, and without warning, the coaster went into the mouth of the dragon, giving me the feeling that it's white fangs were going to bite me, and that the red glow of the dragon's fire was going to burn me. The tempo increased as we passed through the dragon and into the tunnel that was his body. The noise of the tracks and riders' screams made me think that surely this was the end.

Not being able to contain my fear, a loud scream came out of me, causing Michael to stop laughing. I really didn't want Michael to think I was a coward, but I honestly didn't care. I was scared. Thankfully, the ride ended.

When the attendant came to release the safety bar, I just sat there. Michael got out—no problem. The ride didn't faze him. I could see he was still laughing at me. "Come on, Anthony. Get the hell out of the car. Let's go get some soda."

As I got out of the car, my legs were shaking a little. But my sense of urgency to use the bathroom made me race to the restroom near the coaster. I thought for sure I was going to pee in my pants. Come to think of it, maybe that's why they put the bathrooms so close to the coasters.

We all compared our ride experience. None would admit they were afraid some of time. But when they asked me, I didn't care what they thought. With the coaster roaring behind us, I told them. "There's no way in hell you're ever gonna get me on that thing again!"

Everyone laughed. But no one dared call me a chicken. They could see I was in no mood.

With everyone sharing the excitement of the roller coaster ride, Johnny saw an opportunity to get everyone back on track. "OK, guys. Let's go home. Tomorrow, we start work on the fort again. We should all meet there at 10:00 a.m. Agree?"

Between the excitement of the rides and the summer heat, we were quite raunchy looking. Sand was lodged in our bathing suits, creating a very uncomfortable scraping feeling between our legs. Our faces were streaked with dirt marks. We looked like we could use a good bath.

As we approached our bikes, Michael said, "This damn sand is caught between my legs, and it's irritating the hell out of me. Let's go take a shower before we go home. They're building new homes on Oakland Avenue. Anthony and I sneaked into them last week when we went to the beach, and we took a shower on our way home."

We all agreed and sped off to the new subdivision. When we got there, Michael and I showed everyone how to jimmy the windows to get in. We entered two of the houses. Once inside, we stripped down, took cold showers and washed our bathing suits. No sooner did we finish and jump out the windows, the building contractor showed up. He got out of the car and was really pissed when he saw us. He looked like Humphrey Bogart, as the character in *Casablanca*. He was unshaven, his face look dirty with had a cigarette hanging from his mouth. He was skinny as a rail but swift as hell. He ran toward us, shouting, "You're the ones who snuck into here last week and left dirty sand in the showers, aren't you? I'm gonna break your asses if I catch you here again I'll take you to the police station and have them lock you up!"

We sped off on our bikes, agitating him even more.. He jumped into his car tried to catch us, but we were too elusive, weaving in and out of yards and eventually hiding behind a brick wall in another subdivision.

In the span of a few hours, the gang had sneaked into two beaches, sifted for money under the boardwalk, experienced the wonders of Playland, and had a good shower on the way home. Our energy level knew no limits.

That night we went to the Fireman's Carnival. It was an annual event every July hosted by the Harrison Fire Department. They held the carnival in an open field next to the New York, New Haven and Hartford Railroad park on Halstead Avenue. The park and the field was a short walk from my house on Parsons Street. Spread throughout the field were brown canvas canopy tents with lights dangling, strung from poles next to the tents. It was a surreal feeling with the layout of the tents lined up in straight formation like a military-style encampment in World War II movies. It just struck me as strange that each tent had a game with prizes, when I had images of military encampments People put their coins on a number, waiting for a spin of the wheel to hopefully choose that number. I would think of the soldiers in the movies that needed tents like those for hospitals or shelter. It didn't take me long to dismiss those thoughts and get caught up in the excitement of the crowds going from tent to tent to play each game. We were only observers enjoying the festive atmosphere. None of us had money to play any of the games. We would watch people playing the games, hoping some would drop a loose coin. Once they left the booth, we would search around the tent before another group came to play.

There was one booth that we observed more than the others. It was in the main tent that was two to three times bigger than the others. It housed a roulette wheel and refreshment area. A popular game was "Over and Under." Players placed their bet on a number. If the wheel came under their number, they won. If it came over, they lost. We watched players pull out dollar bills and coins for hours. We were hoping they dropped some money. As we watched them, the aroma from the hot dogs cooking on the greasy grill drove us crazy. Sometimes we got lucky and a person would lose some change. We would try to play the game with the found money, but the fireman working the booth chased us away. If we had enough money, we did the next best thing and bought a hot dog.

The next day, my brother Johnny and I would go back to the field. The tent flaps were all pulled down making it difficult for anyone to try and get into them before the carnival opened. Johnny and I would cautiously approach the carnival site making sure no one was watching. The tent we were interested in was the main tent that housed the Roulette Wheel and refreshment stand. We went to the back of the tent. I would pull the back wall up just enough for Johnny to sneak under, and he would do the same for me after he got inside.

We had to be careful not to make noise. Once inside, we paused for a couple of minutes. The only sounds were the traffic on Halstead Avenue and the wind brushing against the tent, making a flapping noise. We paused to make sure someone did not hear or see us. We didn't want to get caught. They might think we were there to steal. Our goal was to hide under the "Over and Under" number board and under the refreshment counter to cull the grass for change. We usually were lucky finding some money, sometimes more than a couple of dollars. Other times when we went, some boys had already gotten there before us and stripped the area clean. We would do this every morning until the carnival ended. The money we found was used to play some of the booth games and, of course, buy more hot dogs.

EIGHT

"GOD, HELP ME! "

One night after supper, my brother Johnny pulled me aside with a very serious look. "Anthony, you were kind of scared at the Dragon Coaster. I know of a way you can overcome fear. It's still light out. We'll tell Mom we're gonna meet the boys on Purdy Street to play a little baseball. But I'm going to take you someplace that will help you not to be afraid to ride on the roller coasters."

"Johnny, I don't have to prove anything. I don't care what you think. I'll go only because I don't want you to keep thinking I'm scared."

Agreeing to go was a mistake.

As we walked up our street, it became apparent to me that my brother was planning something far scarier than anything I'd ever thought possible. Whenever Johnny was planning something, he had a quiet somber demeanor that frightened me. The end result of some of his plans only got us into difficult situations with the neighbors or with Mom.

At the beginning of our street was the major thoroughfare, Halstead Avenue. Parallel to it was the Harrison Railroad Station of the New

York, New Haven and Hartford Railroad. We crossed the avenue and went to the entrance of the small park bordering the railroad station.

I chuckled when we reached the edge of the park just before the over-pass walkway. Some of us use to stand on top of the ledge and test our streaming capabilities to see who could pee the furthest and tried to hit the tracks. Other times we would sneak down to the tracks place a coin on a rail. Rarely did we place anything more than a penny. The flattened coin fascinated and scared us—fascinated that it could be flatten so evenly and frightened that we could get hurt. Other times we just sat on the ledge and watched the trains. We used to try to fig-ure out where all the different freight cars were going and that maybe we should jump on one them and take a trip. Fortunately, we never did.

"Johnny, where the hell are we going?" I asked.

Johnny led me down the steps.

The train station was quiet this time of evening during the summer. Only the whisper of a soft wind was heard gently moving and rat-tling the six-by-three-foot wide station sign: HARRISON. Hitched with S-hooks to the roof rafters, two chains linked to each end suspending the sign from the supporting roof beams.

Still not talking, my brother led me to one of the wooden benches. The bench waiting area ran parallel to the tracks. A yellow line on the concrete platform marked the warning point two feet from the tracks, which alerted people that they were too close to the tracks. Going beyond it, a person could be clipped by a train stopping at the station or sucked into the force of an oncoming passenger express or freight train. We sat down, staring at the tracks and watching the station sign slowly move in a forward and backward motion as the wind blew. Looking westward, the tracks were a molten gold, glisten-ing from the setting sun. Looking eastward, they were covered by the evening dusk. The platform led to a stairwell and then to a sidewalk running parallel to Harrison Ave bridge. The street above, crossed over the high-tension, electrified wires that powered the trains. Blocks of concrete stacked upon one another—like the steps of Mayan temples—supported the bridge. A white wooden picket fence ran in a 'Z' pattern to prevent someone from accidentally falling from the stairwell to the tracks.

Why were we here? What does sitting on a bench by the railroad tracks have to do with overcoming fear? At that moment, it hit me— Christ, he has something planned that will be done here at the train station.

Then Johnny finally spoke. He challenged me. "Anthony, climb on each concrete block and hold tightly to the fence until you reach the steel beam of the bridge crossing over the tracks. Touch the beam and then climb back down to the platform."

I was afraid to climb; fearful an oncoming train would suck me into its vacuum and kill me. But I didn't want to be called a coward. Hesitantly, I carefully climbed the bridge support, holding onto the picket fence along the way. It was getting darker, and the golden glow reflecting on the tracks was starting to be replaced by the darkness of early evening.

Johnny egged me on. "Prove it. Prove you're brave. Climb to the top of the bridge and touch the steel beam. Or, are you chicken? No trains are coming, so hurry up!"

As I climbed closer to the top, I noticed the overhead tension wires six feet from my back. Fearful of falling backwards into them, I pressed my trembling body closer to the fence, gripping each rung so tightly that wood splinters became lodged in my hands.

Halfway to the top, I heard a train whistle coming from the east, piercing the silence of the evening. Turning to look over my right shoulder,

I saw it's beaming light moving closer. Faster it came, the noise of the train getting louder and the light larger as it approached the station.

My brother suddenly realized it was a freight train and screamed in panic, "Hold onto the fence as hard as you can!" He looked like a wounded animal, pacing about and not knowing what to do.

I sensed his panic. Frozen against the fence, I turned to my right again, despite the train light burning into my eyes. I leaned my head closer to the fence and closed my eyes, fully expecting to die by the force of suction. I screamed, "God, help me! Help me! Oh, Lord! I'll never do this again!"

The train rattled faster and faster, seeming it seemed like an eternity. The engineer blared the whistle, helplessly warning me. Out of the corner of one eye, I saw his distraught expression. I often wonder what went through that poor engineer's mind that night, thinking he may have killed me.

Suddenly it was gone. Still frozen, trembling with terror, I held onto the fence. I was so scared that my legs were buckling, making me so weak I almost fell to the tracks below.

My brother called up to me, "Are you all right?"

Slowly I answered, "Yes, but I'm gonna kill *you* when I get down."

He was relieved.

Slowly, my composure came back. I began to descend to the platform. My heart was pounding. Anger toward my brother was building. He had me risk my life by giving me a foolish test. He saw it in my eyes. Slowly lifting my right arm and clenching my fist, I swung. But he grabbed my hand and wrapped his arms around me, holding me tightly. "I'm sorry, Anthony," he whispered into my ear.

He held me for a very long time.

The first time I experienced terror and fear was when I was about five years old, I wanted to play with someone, so I wandered away from my house to an apartment building on Purdy Street. Twin brothers my age were playing in the alleyway with an ice pick, sticking it into a piece of wood. I went up to them to see if I could do the same. They agreed. When I sat down next to them, one picked up the ice pick and swung around. Holding his hand in an upright position, he slashed the left side of my face. The slash ran two inches down from my temple barely missing it. I ran away crying and holding my hand over the cut to stop the bleeding. I could hear them laughing as I ran. When I got home, my mother was in shock when she saw all the blood dripping down my face and onto my clothes and rushed me to the doctor. The scar from that cut is still on my face.

My thoughts went back to two other times that the gang challenged one another's bravery and almost got one of us killed.

One winter, we all challenged Marco to test the ice in the marshland lake, egging him on with "Marco has no balls! He's afraid to test the ice," forcing him to save his honor. Angrily he had run onto the ice. Suddenly there was a cracking sound. Marco turned toward us, mouth open, then shouted, "The ice is breaking!" And it did, dropping him up to his waist in the water below. His arms were flailing and reaching to get to the solid ice, only to have it collapse. He was screaming, "Help me! Help me!" But he was too far out for any one of us to reach him. We turned toward one another frantically,, not knowing how we were going to save him. Panic set in. Marco was sinking fast. The swamp muck was pulling him down with each movement. Then I saw a large branch laying right at the edge of the lake. Grabbing it, I ran to the edge of the lake, a put one foot in the water up to my knee, yelling to the others to hold my left arm. I turned my body to the right and slid the branch over to Marco to grab. He grabbed it, and then I pulled with all my might, and held him so he would not sink. Then, Johnny and Frank came and helped me pull Marco to safety.

When he finally got himself composed, he looked up at all of us. "You fucking guys are all nuts! You almost got me killed. If it wasn't for Anthony, I might have died. Jesus Christ, if my parents see me like this, they will kill me and all of you, too. This wasn't funny!"

We rushed him home, wet and cold, making sure that we went through the side door of his house. We did not want his mother to see what had happened.

Another time that winter, we decided to go to Playland even though it was closed. The goal was to walk the Dragon Coaster tracks and go into the dragon. When we got to Playland, we sneaked in by going through the parking lot and jumping over the fence closest to the Dragon Coaster. Once we got to the coaster customer loading area for the cars, we jumped on the catwalk and followed the tracks upward. At first, it seemed like an easy walk because we were protected by the walls in the covered loading area. As we climbed upward on the catwalk, the only thing preventing us from falling below was the thin railing bordering the catwalk. Anyone could easily fall through the opening in the railing and end up below seriously hurt. At the high point, I got dizzy and almost fell over. Johnny grabbed me. Finally, at the top, we looked up in awe at the dragon's mouth.

Suddenly someone yelled, "Hey, what are you kids doing up there? Get down from there before you get hurt!" We could not see who it was, nor did we want to find out. Instead of running back, we ran into the dragon's body, laughing and yelling as our voices echoed bouncing of the walls of the dragon. Then, instead of going back down the catwalk all the way to the coaster loading area where we surely knew trouble awaited us. We decided to go down in the opposite direction, following the tracks to the lowest level, and hide in the park until it was safe to leave.

I know Johnny was grateful that nothing had happened to me during the railroad challenge. That was the second time he must have felt he was going to lose his little brother. The first time was when he saw me get hit by a car.

Johnny had been about a half a block behind me, walking with his friends on our way home after school. I was with my friends, walking ahead of them. One of the guys from another neighborhood, Michael and Marco's cousin Fred, and I were kicking a box. It was a game to see who could kick it the farthest. Fred kicked it out onto Halstead Avenue, that major thoroughfare. I foolishly went after the box, dodging between the parked cars, not seeing the oncoming traffic, I was hit. My brother saw me tossed into the air, landing on the curb between the parked cars.

I was told that I was taken to the hospital, kept a couple of days, and released, but I don't recall being there. I don't remember anything about the accident or the horror of it.

I do remember being confused at finding myself in my mother's bed because the last place I recalled was running after the box between the parked cars. "Mom, what am I doing in your bed?"

My mother's eyes swelled with tears of joy. "*Dio Christi, graci,*" she said and hugged me. She explained that an accident caused a fractured skull, and that she and my brothers had to keep me awake because I kept wanting to sleep, and how worried everyone was because I did not recognize anyone for at least two weeks.

My brother Johnny came into the room and sat next to me. "Anthony, you know I saw you tossed into the air and then disappear. I ran as fast as I could to see what happened. When I got there, your friends and other people had surrounded you. I broke through them and saw you lying there. Blood was oozing from your head, and your eyes were shut. I thought you were dead." He hugged me. Because of the accident and resulting fractured skull, I had to stay home. It was so severe that the doctors notified the school that I could not finish the first grade. They also wanted me to understand that I could not play physical activities with my friends.

As we were leaving the railroad station, we went up the steps to street level overpass. I thought about what just happened and how lucky I was. As another train was approaching, Johnny and I looked through the mesh fencing to the tracks below. When the train passed beneath us, we both realized the danger I had escaped. Turning away from the fencing, we walked home, my brother's arm on my shoulder. "You know, Anthony, you do have guts."

His compliment did little to diminish the realization of how precious life was to me at that instant with the train, but Johnny realized that foolish challenges have consequences—except he soon forgot it a week later.

It was an afternoon after our traditional Sunday dinner of macaroni, meat balls, and a special treat of Millbrook soda. Mom would make about twelve meatballs, two pounds of Ronzoni Ziti, a salad, and a loaf of buttered Italian bread from Marciano's bakery. My brother Sonny had a ravenousness appetite. His face would be down the entire time he ate. Sometimes I would forget what he looked until he finished. He would consume six of the meatballs and almost a pound of macaroni. Mom, Johnny, and I were lucky to have the six meatballs, too, and the remaining macaroni. We watched Sonny in awe, as he rifled down the macaroni and meatballs. My mother smiled with satisfaction knowing how he enjoyed eating. Funny thing was, Sonny never put on any weight.

Usually on a Sunday, our friends—like us—would have the traditional dinner and stay at home with their families. Sundays were so quiet. No one was working, and the stores were not open due to the religious observation of Sunday as a day of rest. You could hear a pin drop. The day moved very slowly. Everyone spent the day at home together. It was boring with nothing to do. This particular day, we asked for Mom's permission to go over the Biscegla's house and hang around with them for the afternoon. We figured that maybe we could play a game of stick ball or just hang around with them on the front porch.

Mom was okay with us going.

When Johnny and I got there, the Bisceglias were not home. When Johnny realized no one was there, he paused and stared at the commercial building being built across from the Bisceglia home.

"Anthony, look at that bulldozer across the street. Let's go and sit inside it and make believe it's a tank. The Bisceglias and their neighbors aren't home. No one will see us."

Separating the building from the street was an eight-foot-high chain link fence with barb wire at the top stretched from one end to another.

"Johnny we can't go in there. If we get caught, the cops will turn us over to Mom, and you know what will happen then!"

"Look, Anthony. It's no big deal! Come on let's go; it should be fun." He ran across the street, grabbed the chain link fence, and hoisted himself over the barb wire. I knew if I went home, Mom would ask, "Where's your brother?" So, I grasped the fence and pulled myself up. When I got to the top and tried getting over the wire, my pants got caught. I reached over, pulled the wire off, cutting my hand, lost my grip and fell to the other side, and landed right on my rear.

Johnny could not contain his laughter. Hearing it, I looked up, and he was sitting in the driver's seat of the bulldozer, urging me to come up. I grabbed the track thread and crawled up to Johnny. When I got there, he said, "Just stand on the track. I want to see if this tractor starts up." And before I could jump off, he turned the key and pushed the start button causing the bulldozer to crash into the wall and almost getting me injured at the same time. He was totally unaware that he could have hurt me when he did this. I was lucky, but the wall was not. It sustained a three foot crack from being hit. He jumped off the tractor, grabbed me, and hoisted me hurriedly, helping me up and over the fence. He was as fast as kangaroo following me over the fence. He hit the ground saying, "Let's get the hell out of here before anyone sees us. And don't tell Mom or Sonny anything about this," as we ran home.

When I went back many years later, the crack in the wall was now a bump, covered up with cement, year after year, each time it showed itself, as it expanded and contracted with the weather. It reminded me of the lesson learned that day: Escaping danger is not something you can plan, but you hope to have the luck to overcome it when it confronts you.

NINE

"I'M FINISHED BEING A LOOKOUT."

We went to the beach most days that July. The cool waters of Long Island Sound along with the pleasures of the amusement park dampened our enthusiasm for building the fort. The beach was fun. But clearing the ground for the fort, working in the summer heat, getting filthy, and never able to quench our thirsts, was a miserable feeling. Now we knew how our Italian ancestors felt. Mom told me that, when they came to America, they were laborers—digging ditches every day, carrying bricks, kneeling and standing all day with the hot sun beating down on them. My mother's father had an ulcerated leg and still went to work every day digging ditches .The ulcerated leg weakened his resistance level. He caught pneumonia and died at the age of forty-eight. I never met him. My grandfather, on my father's side, was a stone mason. I remember him well. When he took my hand, it was swallowed in his. His hands were so hard that I thought they could crush anything. He passed away when he was sixty-five.

> The old Italians in my family would point with their index finger to their forehead or side of the head and repeat, "Antonio, usa la tua testa." ["Anthony, use your head."] Maybe that is why I

always stayed away from hard manual labor and focused on im-
proving myself through education and developing skills needed
in industry.

Toward the end of July, the gang met at the lot on Purdy Street. It became apparent to us that the fort was never going to get built if we kept going to the beach. We were into the third week of July, and the only progress we made was clearing the lot.

Johnny got us on track. "The lot is cleared. The wagons are built. Now all we have left is to prepare the foundation for the walls and the moats. We have to figure a way to get the doors and clapboard from the old warehouse in the swamp without being noticed. Especially by that nosy old lady across the street from my house." Secrecy was paramount.

We developed a plan to disassemble the old warehouse doors from the buildings. The cattail and reeds lining Oakland Avenue were about eight feet high and blocked seeing the warehouses from the street. That worked in our favor by concealing our movements. The fort was going to be 15 x 15 foot. The doors from the warehouse were about 8 x 3 foot. A total of 15 doors were needed. Because the vegetation was thick, scythes were needed to cut the reeds and make a pathway at the far end of Haviland Street and the edge of the swamp. It was well-hidden from the neighbors who might complain and try to stop us or tell our parents and the police.

We met at my house, which was only a block away from the swamp and warehouses, and we put the scythes, hammers, and crowbar flat on the wagons we had constructed.

We approached the cattail and reed line of the swamp at the corner of Oakland and Haviland and surveyed where to enter the swamp without raising the suspicion of neighbors or the police. We came up with the solution on how to hide our movements. In the center at the far end of Haviland Street stood a massive oak tree with a trunk six feet wide in diameter. It cast a dark shade and acted as a natural cover of the swamp marshes. The path would start and there and lead to the warehouses.

The path we made had to be wide enough for the carts. While the path was being prepared, Johnny sent me to edge of the swamp to be a lookout for the police or anyone else from the neighborhood.

Keeping the noise level down was essential. The swamp bordered Haviland and Oakland Avenues. Across the street was Wilding Park. It had a kiddie pool, swings, monkey bars, and a recreation center. Counselors and parents were always present. The last thing we wanted was for one of them to see what we were doing. Fortunately, the old warehouses were not visible because of the cattails and reeds lining Oakland Ave. No one in the park would be able to see us, but they might hear us banging or pulling the doors and plankboards apart. We counted on the noise level in the park to muffle our sounds. To be on the safe side, my brother wanted me to warn them if any of the counselors or parents seemed curious.

When I got to the edge of the swamp, I peered through the reeds and watched the children playing in the park. I thought that it was pretty smart of us to put the path off Haviland Avenue and not to put it across the street from the park. The other fear Johnny and I had was to watch for our Aunt Rosie. Getting caught in the swamps by her would be more serious than if the cops caught us. Every time a car came down Oakland Ave, I would look for her big black 1948 Packard that she and her and my Uncle Joe had bought from a New York City cab company. That car was built like a tank. It could seat eight people. One time when we were walking along the Post Road in Rye, she blared the horn, making us freeze in our tracks. When she stopped the car, she opened the window and yelled with a screeching voice that could rattle plates off a table. "What are you doing in Rye? You should all be in your own neighborhood. Get the hell into the car—all of you. You're going home with me. And, Anthony and Johnny, if I tell your mother, she's going to whack the both of you right on your butts. Now get in all of you!" Johnny had stepped back from the car as he said, "But Aunt Rosie, there isn't enough room for all of us in the car." But she snapped back, "Oh yes, there is. Don't give me any lip. Get in!" That old Packard had pull-down seats fastened to the driver and passenger side for two more passengers. All the way home, she lectured us. She told us she knows everything that we do. Our friends sat quietly in the car, their hands folded on their laps, eyes straight ahead peering through the front window. Not a word was spoken.

She was like a telegraphist. No matter where we went, somehow she knew and if she knew our parents would get the message. We never knew where she was patrolling.

One time, Johnny and I were by the railroad tracks. When we got home, Mom stopped us. "What were you doing by the railroad tracks this afternoon?"

We had no phone, so how did Mom find out?

Johnny looked at me and then to her and asked, "Mom, did Paul Revere send you the message that we were at the railroad tracks?"

"Never mind who told me! Don't go there again!"

We figured it was Aunt Rosie; she was like a sleuth.

Our aunt had a strong personality. She was about five-feet-three and stocky. Her square chin and high cheek bones gave her a stern look. She was stubborn, strict, and always straight to the point. She was the youngest of my father's sisters. There were many times while we were growing up, she would pop up out of nowhere—especially when we were in places where we should not have been. And my Uncle Joe, her husband, would come to our house at least once a month and sit with us for a couple of hours. He was short, quite muscular, and had fair hair and a light complexion like me. He loved to talk politics.

> *My brothers and I learned a lot from Uncle Joe. One time I asked him, "Uncle Joe, how come the papers and people on the radio always make all Italians feel ashamed because of the Mafia." I'll never forget his response: "Anthony, don't be ashamed to be Italian. The Italians have done great things in America. Those people that talk about the Mafia rarely mention the other mafias in the world. Every nation has criminals like the mafia. And other ethnic groups in our country have them. Most people are good no matter where they are, and they don't belong to criminal groups. So, when someone tells you it's only the Italians, stick up for yourself. Tell them what I just told you. You'll see when you get older how right I am." And he was.*

Mom would make him tea and put two bags and fill a large tea bowl with hot water. I would rest my head on both hands with my arms leaning on the table and watch him yank the tea bag like a yo-yo while he talked to us and sipped the tea until the bowl was empty. My brothers and I respected both him and Aunt Rosie. They cared enough to be concerned for our well-being and checked on us ever since the time our father passed away. Aunt Rosie, with her constant patrols and the fear of her wrath, insured we did not get in trouble, and Uncle Joe, spent the time with us, talking to us about life in general.

Aunt Rosie did patrol Oakland Ave that day. She must have cruised the neighborhood and, not seeing us, thought to check by the swamp. She and our parents knew how dangerous it was to go near the old warehouses that were sinking into the swamp. Their wood frames were rotting at the base. If they listed to the right, and their collapse was imminent.

When I saw her, I laid down in the reeds totally hidden by the dense reeds. If she saw me, we would all be dead.

During that time on watch, the mosquitoes were having a feast. One after another, they bit me on my face, mostly my forehead. They bit me on my legs, too, and the itching became almost unbearable. My concealed position was in danger of being exposed by my restless movements. I thought, if Aunt Rosie saw the reeds and cattails moving, she might stop to investigate.

I was getting anxious to get up and leave. Then something was crawling up my leg. I thought it was a copperhead. "Please get off me," I silently pleaded, beginning to panic.

Now I had a dilemma. If I got up, I would no longer be concealed. The counselors at the park would see me, as well as my Aunt Rosie driving by in the car.

I crawled backward farther into the reeds and then ran in a crouched position through the reeds toward the opening where the warehouses were. When I got there, I used a pointed stick to lift my pant leg, anticipating that the snake would be on my leg. I was ready to kill it with my pocketknife.

Looking down at my leg, I began to laugh.

I was laughing so hard I fell down on the ground. The copperhead turned out to be a reed that got caught on the inside of my dungaree. The fear about the snakes that had been instilled in us had raged hell with my imagination.

Lying in the swamps really sucks in the summer. I liked the swamps in the winter when we can skate on the frozen creek all the way up to Mamaroneck and play hockey on the pond.

It was more fun than summer with all the mosquitos and having to worry about getting bit in the rear or leg by a snake and itching all day from the mosquito bites. The best part of winter in the swamps was when we built a bonfire on the lake after the hockey games to warm us.

I told my brother, "I'm finished being a lookout. Send somebody else." Then I joined the rest of the gang working on the warehouses.

The warehouse buildings were built in the thirties. There were three rows of buildings made of wooden clapboard construction and shaped like barracks. They were once a printing plant that produced sheet music: "American Patrol," "Ten Little Soldiers on a Ten-Day Leave," and "Don't Sit under the Apple Tree." The four-page song booklets were damp and mildewed, sticky to the touch. Now, scattered about as the wind blew through one end of the dilapidated warehouse to the other, my friends stepping on them as they worked on tearing the doors off the metal tracks.

I thought of the times that those abandoned buildings were once filled with people coming to work. I would imagine them there singing the songs they printed. I pictured those workers reading the lyrics and dancing to them, as they printed and packed them for distribution. Where were those people now? What happened to them? Did they die in the war? Sometimes, when the breeze rattled the hanging doors and brushed the swamp reeds along the side of the buildings, I would get a weird feeling as if they were watching. I wondered if someday we were going to fade like them and those song sheets, that were cast about in aimless disarray? Will someone tear apart everything we built?

My thoughts came back to the gang as they were dismantling the doors. The doors hung on a track. We opened one end of the track letting the doors slide to the ground and then took apart the loose clapboards, prying them off with a crowbar.

Care had to be taken not to damage the doors. They were going to be the main walls. They would be put in the foundation trench dug at the lot. The clapboard was going to be used to tack the doors together, making the walls stronger to withstand external force by a battering ram—just in case. Some of the pieces would be used to complete portions of the wall where we didn't have enough doors.

Using the doors for walls ended up saving us a lot of time. Otherwise, we would have had to create a framed wall for the entire fort. The useable nails that we salvaged were put into an empty Prince Albert pipe tobacco can. They would be used with the clapboard. The collection of doors and clapboard was put into piles on the pathway made earlier, positioned for loading on the carts. Watching the gang dismantle the doors and clapboard looked like a movie in reverse. Instead of the doors being positioned to stay on, they were taken down. Instead of the clapboard being nailed to a frame for a wall, they were being ripped out of the wall. The gang worked with little regard for the splinters, hammer hits on the thumb, or scratches on their arms. They kept at it, driven by the desire to build the fort. No one took a break.

Finally, "OK, guys. Let's take a break," Johnny said.

We all sat in a circle. We were a grimy looking bunch, with sweaty dirt streaks running down our faces, our clothes smudged with the black muck of the swamp. My arms and legs were aching from helping to dismantle the doors..

Johnny motioned like he was holding a cigarette. He asked, "Michael, do you have any of your old man's cigarettes?"

Pulling out a pack of Parliaments, Michael gave each of us a cigarette. Smoking was a reward. We likened it to a slogan on the Camel cigarette poster advertisements: *I'd walk a mile for a Camel*. We mimicked Humphrey Bogart with cigarettes hanging out of our mouths as we talked.

Looking back to those moments of smoking, I can still see a bunch of boys blowing smoke out of their mouths, puffing circles like the old billboard in Times Square.

After the break, we had to move the doors and clapboard to the lot on Purdy Street without arousing suspicion in the neighborhood. It took us four days to do this without anyone seeing us. Moving the materials was like a cat and mouse game. Every car that passed, we jumped, nervous that someone would stop and question us.

TEN

"WADDA YOU BOYS WANT TODAY?"

As I look back to that summer, I often wonder if we were an enigma. While schoolmates were going to the beaches or traveling with families, we were immersed in constructing the fort. The physical effort to build it was exceptional for boys of our age.

When we brought the doors to the fort site, the ingenuity of the plan converting the doors to walls made the fort a reality. We took each door and laid it outside the footprint and foundation trenches for the four walls. Five doors for each side were fastened with strips of clapboard to hold them together. When the doors were connected, they were lifted and slid into a foundation trench which then was backfilled with stone and dirt to ground level.

The walls were made stronger with two-by-four studs. The braces were nailed at a forty-five degree angle to the doors to provide support and withstand anyone trying to knock down the walls.

We would work until we couldn't lift another door or hammer. We wanted this fort completed before summer was over. Sandlot baseball was on hold until we finished. We became captives of the fort.

Finally, in the middle of August as we were putting together the front wall which would be the last one, we realized that one more door was needed to complete it. Otherwise there would be an opening anyone could get in. Panic ensued. There were no doors left at the old warehouses. We sat there trying to figure out what to do.

Then Marco burst out with, "Hey, I know where we can get a door. On my way home from the Five & Dime the other day, I saw some guys take a freezer door out of Mrs. Polomenta's store. She might not mind if we take it. The damn thing is huge. It'll take up the opening and be a lot stronger than the walls. But it will take six of us to move the door."

"And how are we going to hinge it?" my brother asked.

Grabbing a stick, Marco then formed the shape of a hole with his left index finger and thumb and inserted the stick into it. "Look, it has two round hinges that we can place a pipe in, so the door can swing open or shut."

"OK, let's go get the door," Johnny said.

The six of us went to Mrs. Polementa's store. She was standing in the doorway of the store with a hand fan to fend off the heat of that hot summer day and wearing the same blue polka dot dress and white apron for work every day.

> I remember her as a kind person. She was portly and short. Her graying hair was always pulled back and tied into a bun. Her olive complexion was as smooth as silk, and she had charming blue eyes. She was kind and very patient with us.

We usually bought penny candy there. Sometimes, when we couldn't get cigarettes from Mr. Bisceglia's stock, we would buy them from her. She would sell them in singles. When she asked who the cigarettes were for, one of us would allege that they were for an adult.

Each time we went into the store, she always greeted us with a smiling sense of resignation, watching us as we rambled through the store, observing us with a distrustful look, suspicious of our motives. With one eyebrow up, she'd ask, "Wadda you boys want today?" She stopped fanning herself and put both hands on her hips in a defensive posture.

Marco went up to her to try to convince her that, since she was throwing away the freezer door, would she mind if we took it.

With a cynical look and her hands still on her hips, she said something like this in broken English, "And wadda you gonna do with it?"

Mrs. Polementa's store was right next to the police station. The last thing we wanted her to do was tell them she gave us the door for a fort. So, we did what we were good at and manufactured another story, telling her we were going to try to peel back the metal and sell some of it to the junkman so we can get some money."

I don't think she believed us. But she knew we were kids that had very little money so she agreed we should have it.

Three of us got on each side of the door and lifted it. Moving in sync, our goal was to carry it to the fort which was about five blocks from the store. Along the way, the weight of the door shifted toward my side and almost fell on me, Michael, and my brother Johnny. We wobbled a little but were able to regain our footing.

We crossed the thoroughfare at Harrison Ave and Colonial Street by the firehouse. As we crossed the street and walked by the firehouse, the one thing we worried about was if the fire alarm would going off and the trucks come roaring out.

Johnny yelled, "Hurry up! Concentrate! We have to get out of the way in case the fire alarm goes off! Hold onto the door tighter, look straight ahead. Don't look anywhere else!"

We finally got the door to the fort and dropped it on the ground. We all sat down relieved. We nervously laughed at how we must have looked carrying a freezer door across one of the major street thoroughfares.

Afterward, we positioned the freezer door and built the foot ramps to each wall. Then we chopped down an eighteen-foot tree and stripped the branches and bark to create a pole. On top of the pole, we built a three-by-three-foot platform and braced it to that pole. Next, we nailed wood rungs onto it for a ladder, creating our lookout tower.

"OK, carry the lookout tower and anchor it to the center of the fort" said my brother John" then put it into the three-foot hole."

Some of the cynics in the gang gave him a look of uncertainty, unsure whether the pole would stay in the hole, feeling it would not and that it would come down on us.

It took all six of us to carry the pole. Before we placed it into the hole, we tied two twenty-five-foot rope lines to the center and top. We angled the bottom into the hole, pushing the top upward until we could no longer reach it.

"Push! Push!" Johnny yelled until we gained the upper hand.

Michael and I were the shortest of the gang. When we could no longer help with pushing the pole, we let go of it and grabbed the ropes. We pulled the pole upward until the others could help us after they also let go of the pole. We could feel its weight pulling us forward. We held on and kept it stable while the others backfilled the hole with dirt and rocks to secure the lookout tower.

The tower was now in place. We all stood around the pole and looked up at it in awe that we could put something so tall in the ground and that it remained standing. It was like looking at the flag when the national anthem is played.

I remember feeling a sense of pride in that final day when we put up the tower. We had achieved a magnificent feat of construction. Grimy and dirty from the sap of the pole, cuts on our hands and scratches on our arms, we turned toward each other and grinned. It was one of those rare moments when I knew something great had happened.

With the lookout tower sturdy, the roof could be laid, and the inside foot walk added, completing the final construction of the fort.

One night, there was a fierce thunderstorm and strong winds. Looking out the windows at home, we saw the trees in the neighborhood swaying like Hula dancers. Branches were flying all over, with some trees crashing down in the middle of the street. All Johnny and I could think of was the possibility of the walls of the fort collapsing and the tower crashing down.

The next morning, we rushed through breakfast and ran to the fort, hoping it would be standing but expecting it would not.

"Look, Johnny! Everything's fine," I said.

The rest of the gang met us, also expecting the fort to not be there. "Yeah! Yeah, the fort lives! Look, the rainwater washed more dirt into the foundations and reinforced the walls and tower."

It was like a divine power blessed the fort with greater strength.

The storm reinforced our feelings of invincibility. We felt that nothing could destroy the fort. Our next goal was to finish the fort by putting a roof over it and finish the inside foot-walk along the wall edges, using planks from Marco and Michaels father's construction yard. Then we laid other planks across the top of the walls to form a flat roof. Over the planks, we laid corrugated tin sheets and other scraps of metal and wood that we found at the old warehouses.

Defensive openings one foot wide were cut three per wall to position slingshots. Next, we cleaned out the scraps from the construction on the inside and compartmentalized an area for each of us. Our room away from home, the only thing we left out was window openings, but light from the slingshot outlooks gave us ample illumination.

Finally, it was finished. Slowly each of us filed out and gathered in front of the fort. We stood together with one arm over each other's shoulder, chest bursting with pride. We each raised an arm, loudly exclaiming, "The fort is finished! The fort is finished!"

Our shouts could probably be heard throughout the neighborhood until Johnny halted the celebration. "Great job, men. But we have one more thing to do—the moat. We have to dig it around the fort and fill it with stuff that will stop intruders. We'll go around and collect some dog dung and fill the moat with it, along with wood spikes and glass. And we'll cover-up the moat with branches and grass. That'll teach anyone who tries to get in."

His reasoning for the moat was that, if we were not there, the moat would guard the fort and, if we were there, the moat would protect us from attack. Anyone not familiar with the moat locations would fall in and startled deterring them from trying to get into it.

Johnny wasn't too popular after insisting that the moat be finished. Bitching and moaning, we dug the moat and filled it with obstacles. It must have taken a half day to finish the moat. Tired, hot, sweaty, thirsty and hungry, casting our shovels aside and dropping to the ground, we lay there, silently staring at the clouds, too tired to talk. The joy of finishing the fort earlier was suppressed by the fatigue of digging the moats.

We perked up when we heard the sound of the Good Humor truck. What better way to reward ourselves, we thought, than with an ice-cold ice cream.

The Good Humor man's first name was Freddy. He loved conversing with us about sports and had an interest in some of our activities. He used to stop for a cigarette where they stacked the milk cartons in a small parcel at the bottom of the Purdy street. We always looked for Freddy in the summer because that meant ice cream bars. Sometimes we had money to buy, but most times we did not. Sometimes when he had extra ice cream, he would give us a free bar.

We waited for the tinkle of the Good Humor truck to get closer. As it turned the corner onto Purdy street, we could see the white truck with a giant chocolate and vanilla ice cream bar painted on the sides. Our mouths watered at the thought of eating the delicious bars. Freddy always kept his truck meticulously clean and his white uniform was pressed, military style. The money-changer hooked on the front of his black belt. The white hat had a black peak and gold rope band that reminded me of a US Naval officer.

Freddy was a small-built narrow faced man and snow-white gray hair. He wore gold rim sunglasses. When he took the sunglasses off, his sky-blue beautiful eyes were revealed. He had a habit of squeezing his right hand, as if he had something in it.

Sometimes when we begged or pestered him for free ice cream, he would tell us to line up, one abreast and he'd throw a few bars at us and watch us fight over them, chuckling the whole time. "When are you kids ever going to learn to share?"

Freddy finally arrived and parked his truck, got out of the driver's seat and sat on the step of the truck, pulled out a pack of Lucky Strikes, lit a cigarette and blew out a puff of smoke. He could see we were waiting for him. "Hi, boys. What are you up to today? I hear you are building a fort in the woods behind the cave. How's it going?"

"Mr. Freddy..." That's the way we addressed him since we did not know his last name. "...we just finished it," Johnny said.

"Wow! You guys built that pretty fast! So, what are you doing hanging around here by the milk cartons? Are you waiting for me?"

"Look, Mr. Freddy, we have been working hard all day and we were thinking that maybe you would be kind enough to give us some ice cream."

Freddy flicked the ash from his cigarette, and then he looked us over, shaking his head right to left in thought on how to respond. "Free? Look, I can't give you free ice cream. The company will fire me."

Disappointed, we started to move away.

He never used harshness in his voice, but this time, he could see that his response affected us.

Freddy shouted, "Come back here, I have an idea. I'll do this. I can give you three more free ones, which I'll pay for, but that's all I can do or afford. Which means you will have to share them."

"Ah crap, Freddy, that means three of us have to share three ice cream sticks. Why not just give us three Popsicles, and we can break them up and have one each? That way everybody gets something." It was a brilliant solution by Johnny.

Freddy reached into the ice cream truck and pulled out three ice popsicles. Watching him reach into the cold freezer and handing them to us, I noticed how red his right hand was from the continued reaching into the freezer. Maybe that was the reason he often squeezed his right hand.

He was one of the nicest people that we ever met. Kind heart and always with a smile. Every once in a while, when I have an ice cream cone or bar on a hot summer day, Freddy in his white

uniform appears, smiling as he enjoys watching me devour an
ice cream.

We all parted to head home for supper, savoring the popsicle that completed a day of accomplishments.

Michael & Marco Bisceglia   Anthony & John Matero   Bobby & Frank Sollazzo

THE PURDY STREET GANG

Purdy Street Field-Once Was

Sollazzo Apartment Building

Where The Mountain Once Stood

Hill Where the gang did the night of the Boy Scout meeting.

Fence by Cemetery

Where The Fort once Stood

Church Exit

Swamp

Playground opposite Warehouses

The Swamp Creek. Note: the Fence on left is where the warehouses once stood.

Dragon Coaster

Photos by Louis Alfieri

Where we climbed into the Dragon's Mouth

Rye Playland Carousel and Caramel Outside Road Jumper- Photos by John Caruso

Fence where I hung on as the train approached

Biltmore Theatre

Halstead Ave. (Parsons Memorial) School

Christopher Columbus

Amelia Earhart Monument

World War I
Soldier Monument

Frank P. Sollazzo Recreation Center
Center was formerly the "Aranac"

Mr. Sollazzo

Basketball Court in Center

Our House On Parson Street

Mom, Johnny, Me
&
Blackie

Earlier Photo
Johnny, Mike (Sonny in the book) and Me

Mr. & Mrs. Bisceglia-
Note Fedora Hat & Cigarette

Marco, Michael & Jerry – Pigeon Coop Built Similar to Ours

Sollazzo Family

ELEVEN

"OK, GUYS. YOU KNOW THE PLAN!"

The Gang had a fondness for causing trouble in a mischievous way. When the fort was finished, the dream to have our own hangout became a reality. The entire month of July we were driven to complete it. With the construction task completed, we now had the luxury of time to dream. The fort became the devil's workshop.

Every day, as soon as we had eaten breakfast, my brother and I rushed out of the house to pick up Michael and Marco on our way to the fort. The four of us raced up the hill. I can still see the smiles on everyone's faces as we ran up the hill. We pushed one another to the side, trying to be the first one to the top yelling, "The last one up the hill is a rotten egg!"

We sat down on the wooden fruit crates taken from the First National Grocery Store's garbage bin. We were free from the daily control of our parents, feeling secure that they were out of earshot of our conversations and rascally plans. We enjoyed being with one another. Our language was becoming a mix of good upbringing and roughneck gang language. We were getting bolder. As we sat around the fort that summer, our minds would wander. We would also think of ourselves as great adventurers or soldiers trying to correct the ills of the world. We were zealots, determined to right the wrongs.

I'm amazed at the number of events that transpired from our conversations in the fort during the final weeks of vacation. Each is a story unto itself:

Milton Point in Rye, New York

We went to the marina on Milton Point during the weekdays when most of the boat owners were gone. Our plan was to take the beached dinghies out to their yachts. The boat owners took precautions not to leave the oars in the dinghies. For the oars, we used flat boards from the fruit cartons or clapboard and tied them to our bikes.

The bike ride was about the same distance as Playland. The marina had very little security. To be on the safe side, three of us checked the dock building to make sure no one was around. Once we determined it was safe, we hid our bikes, loosened the moorings, and rowed the dinghies out to the yachts. The whiteness of the yachts was brilliant. The blinding sunlight hitting the sides of them and reflecting off the glistening water made it difficult for us to row in a straight path. When we got to the yachts, we climbed up on the decks from the mooring rope on their sides. Then we laid on our backs, absorbing sun and, when it became too hot, we dove into the water.

With all of us gathering on one boat, it looked like a party—some of us standing and talking and others laying on their backs, while others dove into the water. After we borrowed those yachts a couple of times, the boat owners increased security by having someone check on the marina. We had to get off the boats whenever we saw what we thought was the harbor master's car pull up. Panicked, we thought for sure he would call the police. Everyone on deck got inside the cabin, hoping he would not see us. The others stayed on the opposite side of the yacht facing the harbor. No one made any noise. An eerie silence came over us, fearing we would be caught. We knew that he could not see the dinghies because they were tied to the side that couldn't be seen from the shore. We waited for what seemed like hours for some movement from the harbor master. Finally, he turned the car around and drove off. One at a time, we slipped over the side to the dinghies and rowed fast to the shore like oarsmen of a rowing team. Once on shore, we tiptoed quietly to our bikes and rode off, hoping no one was around waiting for us. Lucky for us if we did not get caught or we would be in deep trouble with the owners of the boats and the Rye cops.

The Movies

Going to the movies required money, which most times we did not have. A good source of money was collecting empty soda and beer bottles. Sometimes on my way home from school, I would collect the empties and set them aside, bringing them to the stores on the weekend for the deposit money.

> Collecting beer and soda bottles in the late forties and early fifties was like looking for gold in the Sahara Desert. Most people held onto them for getting the deposit money back.

On Saturday mornings, the gang would split up and hunt for discarded glass bottles. Most times, we had better luck finding empty bottles by road construction sites or behind gas stations. We always put the bottles into paper bags, the stench of the stale beer growing stronger with each bottle we collected.

"God, who drinks this crap? It smells like urine when it hits the fire" was often my opinion of the aroma.

My friend Michael would correct me often. "No, Anthony. It's not the beer that stinks. It smells like somebody took a leak in some of the bottles."

The sticky soda bottles left a syrup residue on our hands, and dirt lined our palms. We often rubbed our hands against our dungarees to remove the annoying mess. Our mothers were not very happy about that. In those days, they washed everything by hand on a scrubbing board. My mother's upper biceps would swell as she scrubbed our clothes, standing over the kitchen sink for what I thought was hours. Many a time when we got out-of-hand, Johnny and I caught the power of those arms with a quick whack across our butts or shoulders.

After scouting for bottles, we brought them to the First National grocery store for the deposit money. I always enjoyed the exasperated look of the clerks when we walked into the store. When we arrived with the empty bottles, they grudgingly them, picked them up by the neck of the bottle to avoid the sticky residue and dirt. We never cleaned them, and you could tell they were upset with us.

The movie theater was only a few blocks from our neighborhood. The daring plan for all of us to get into the movies was designed by Johnny. We would collect just enough money for two of us to gain admission to the Biltmore Theater. The two selected to purchase tickets were Michael and me. The plan was for us to position ourselves in the theater, close to the side emergency fire exit doors. The others would be outside by the door, waiting for us to push the doors open. When we pushed the doors open they would run inside the theater going in different directions and mix with the paying patrons.

I was never really comfortable with crashing into the movie theater, yet I kind of relished the challenge. Plus, I wanted to see movies like

John Wayne in Iwo Jima with his heroic acts of bravery, Ester Williams in her bathing suit, and the cartoons like Mighty Mouse and Bugs Bunny.

One Saturday, when we got to Marco and Michaels house, we stopped cold in our tracks.

"Shit!" I said. "Mr. Bisceglia is cutting his hedges!"

He reminded me of Edward G. Robinson—short, stocky, and tough, but better-looking. He would move the hedge cutter with its disk-shaped blade which looked like a flying saucer hovering over the hedges as it clipped them, miraculously missing the electric wire of the hedge cutter with each swipe. He took a lot of pride in them. The bushes looked like they had been taken care of by professional landscapers. He always wore a long-sleeved shirt, even on the hottest summer days, along with a gray fedora hat topped by a feather, sweat beading down the sides of his face. While cutting, moving from left to right, he always had a Parliament cigarette hanging from the corner of his mouth. Yet the ash hanging from the cigarette never fell as he cut the hedges and talked.

Johnny and I were scared to death of him. He was one tough character, as evidenced from the stories told by Marco and Michael of his disciplinary ways.

He had a knack for extracting information. We rarely engaged in conversation with him for fear of a slip-up. His bark had a forewarning to it, but rarely did he ever result to physical means. Confronting him before picking up Marco and Michael always required choosing our words carefully. Whenever we approached him, I would let Johnny do the talking. Honestly, from me he would get the real reasons of what our plans were for a particular day.

"What are you going to do, Johnny?" I asked.

"Be quiet. Let me do the talking," he said. "Good afternoon, Mr. Bisceglia."

"*Buon giorno,* Antonio and Giovanni. *Come stai?*"

"*Bene, bene.*"

"Michael and Marco are on the porch waiting for you." Then, in his prying manner, cigarette hanging with the ash intact, one eyebrow up and a half smile, he said, "Hmm, boys. Tell me, how did you get the money for the movies?"

He pulled the cigarette from his mouth, flicking the ashes to the ground. This time, both eyebrows were pointed, and the smile had turned to a clenched lip. The inquisitor at work.

My brother Johnny told him we got the money by returning soda and beer bottles and getting reimbursed for their deposit.

"Ah, I see."

I could tell it wasn't enough of an answer for him.

"Johnny, where did you bring the bottles for deposit?"

"We brought them to the First National on Halstead Avenue."

Satisfied with our answer, he flipped the cigarette to the ground, pointing his index finger while grinding the discarded cigarette, he waved us toward the house and resumed his yardwork.

After Michael and Marco joined us, we went on to meet the others at the field on Purdy Street.

Johnny said, "OK, guys. You know the plan. Michael and Anthony will open the doors once the cartoons start, and we'll all rush in. Just make sure nobody gets caught."

The Biltmore was two blocks away. The front of the building and the ticket booth were on Harrison Avenue, and the side of the movie theater stretched back almost to Purdy Ave. The rest of the gang broke off from me and Michael to access the alleyway through the ramp leading to the back of the theater.

As Michael and I approached the Biltmore, my heart raced in anticipation of the new movie that was advertised for the weekend. I focused on the marquee, looking at the words and hoping it was one of my favorite movie stars or characters: John Wayne, Roy Rogers, Tarzan, Flash Gordon, Gene Autry, or Esther Williams. I also wondered what kind of cartoons would be playing. Would they be Mighty Mouse, Buggs Bunny, Daffy Duck, or Tom and Jerry?

The excitement built until we got to the veranda where we studied the movie posters on exhibition in glass cases and imagined ourselves as one of the characters: John Wayne defending America as a Marine platoon leader during World War II or Randolph Scott in the *Nevadan*. Randolph Scott, I like a lot. I favored him more than the other actors because I compared him to my father's image. My father looked a lot like him. Each movie I saw with Randolph Scott and hearing his voice, the image of my father would appear in my mind, and I would wonder if this was how my father's voice sounded?

Michael and I handed our money to the owner of the theater, Mr. Tommasino, who was sitting in the ticket booth, pushing tickets. He always wore a suit and tie. His theater was a reflection of him—well-kept and clean.

Once in the theater, we sat close to the exit door.

I can still see that stage, maroon curtains and gold tassels stretching across the entire length. Red carpeting flowed down the aisles and floors. Maroon paper covered the walls. A chandelier hung from an arched ceiling, with bowed, hand-plastered beams following its contour. Each beam held sculptures of different flowers that were artfully spaced between each other. The varnished floors under the seats were worn from years of use, but the red velvet seats were still comfortable. They were so delightful that, after the movies, I often wanted to close my eyes and go to sleep.

The theater lights dimmed, the newsreel of current events began, followed by the cartoons. We slowly got up from our seats, looking for Mr. Tommasino or his ushers. We were very nervous. As we walked to the exit door, we constantly turned to watch the other kids in case one of them bolted to tell Mr. Tommasino what we were about to do. The hair on the nape of my neck felt like it was sticking straight out. Fearing we would be caught, I wanted to run back to my seat but forged on anyway. As soon as *Mighty Mouse* started on the screen, we pushed down on the exit door bar, releasing the doors to the outside. Everyone in the theater looked toward the door. We were saved by the outside light beaming into the darkened theater, blinding everyone momentarily and providing the rest of the gang outside with the opportunity to rush in. They fanned out in different directions in the theater.

The audience was yelling, "Shut the door! Shut the door!"

Poor Mr. Tommasino rushed toward the doors, closing them and mumbling his anger. If he caught us, we would be barred from entering the movie theater. But he had little chance of catching us. Once he closed the doors, he went aisle to aisle looking for the culprits. He flashed his light in kids' faces, trying to detect the slightest hint of the intruders. One time he flashed the light in my face. I raised my hand to block the beam and kept staring at the movie screen. I felt like jumping up and running, but I stayed seated, almost wetting my pants in fear of being caught. After the movie, we all met outside and nervously laughed it off. Eventually Mr. Tommasino had enough and positioned an usher at the exit doors every Saturday matinee.

As a group being quite close, we all had very active and similar imaginations. The movies we saw inspired us. We had a playbook of sorts. One day, we were Marines fighting the enemy. Another day, we were Tarzan, flying from limb to limb in the weeping willows at Beaver Pond, screaming his ape-like howl. Then we were pushing our rafts in the streams to the marsh banks, jumping off them the way we imagined Marines jumping from amphibious vehicles, singing the chorus, "*From the Halls of Montezuma....*" We were pointing our makeshift rifles made from wood scraps, firing our imaginary weapons, and imitating the sounds of bullets with our throats as we moved through marshes and reeds looking for imaginary enemies.

Our playbook became very different with Esther Williams. When she came on the screen with her narrow jawline, shoulder-length hair, soft eyes and shapely figure, we were silenced. We sat motionless, staring at her. She was like a Roman goddess, stirring unexplained feelings in each of us. We watched her dolphin-like skills in awe. She dove, flying downward with her arms stretched back at her sides, an arrow plunging into the waters below, then surfacing with a smile, arms outstretched over her head, arching and bowing her body in an upward motion for a backward flip.

Esther Williams gave us confidence to overcome our fear of water and enjoy it at Oakland Beach. We mimicked her swimming positions. We became strong swimmers at an early age, thanks to Esther Williams.

One movie that left an impression with all us was *The Thing*, a story about an alien creature whose spaceship crashed in the arctic circle and was locked in the frozen ice. Throughout the movie, we all sat scared out of our wits. James Arness played this giant creature with hands the size of elephant feet and a head with bumps the size of an orange on each side. Once they defrosted him, he was destructive and virtually unstoppable. My brother Johnny, throughout the movie, saw how frighten I was, came close to my ear and whispered "boo" throughout the movie causing me to jump with fear. When the movie was over, I ran away from him. I rushed to the path that went along the Sollazo apartment building and hid from him in the alleyway. Because it was starting to get dark, Johnny began whistling, concealing his own nervousness from the movie. As soon as he got to the point of the alleyway and the path, I jumped out in front of him and yelled so loudly that his hair went straight up, "Boooooo!" I ran away as fast as I could, laughing all the way home, gleeful that the score was even for his scaring me during the movie. Once he regained his composure, he bolted after me, but I beat him home. When he got there, he just gave me that I'll-get-even look.

Years later, when I was decades older, I went back and walked along Halstead Avenue and crossed to Harrison Avenue where the Biltmore Theater still stands. The street and buildings haven't changed in character since I was a boy.

The buildings, on that strip of Harrison Avenue were designed in the late twenties, some probably built by Italian masons. In many ways, they looked like the movie sets of westerns. Each had distinctive elements, with brick facades or stucco. Some had flat roofs or tile overhangs.

Like all small theaters of its day, the Biltmore has yielded to today's multiplex theaters. Today, it stands empty, all alone on a once busy street filled with moviegoers and shoppers. Mr. Tommasino always kept it in immaculate condition. Its marquee, once a beacon of invitation with its large letters advertising the movies of the week, is now rusting away. Back then, it lured us to fill our imaginations with grandeur and adventure. The arcade with its glass poster cases is empty now. Gone are our heroes. The theater doors show the grime from the busy traffic on Harrison Avenue. The back of the theater and the alleyway, where the gang waited to sneak in, was littered with garbage bags and debris. Once a majestic temple of adventure, hope, and daring to a neighborhood gang of boys, the Biltmore has slowly tarnished and faded, along with our many exploits.

Girls

Our parents never knew most of the things we did—cigarette smoking, our curiosity about the opposite sex, sometimes looking in magazines that showed us their anatomy—magazines like the *Sears Roebuck Catalog* and *National Geographic Magazine.* The first time I ever saw a partially naked woman was in a *National Geographic.* The photos led us to have conversations about the girl that lived across the street from my house.

She was around Johnny and Frank's age, maybe a few months older. She had blond hair, fair complexion, gray blue eyes, and was about 5 feet 4. We all thought she looked like some of the models with her striking physical features. At 13, almost 14, she was fully developed and very pretty. When she crossed the street on the way to meet the other girls in the neighborhood, her ponytail bobbing, I thought that someday she would be just as beautiful as Esther Williams. I wondered what she would look like naked. Would she be like the women in National Geographic? When she saw me staring at her, she gave a smile and said, "Hi, Anthony"

I became breathless.

Sometimes she would inquire about my brother Johnny. I think she liked him. But Johnny was just as shy as me and avoided her.

Something was stirring in me that I could not identify. One day, another girl across the street saw Michael and I playing with the two goats her parents kept in the field next to her house. We used to call her parents "The Goat People." We were pretending to be bull fighters, teasing the goats to charge us. We made sure that we never turned our backs on them. When we finished with our game, Michael went home.

I was crossing the field to head home, too, when she came up to me and motioned me to the apple tree by Michael's house. When I got there, we talked for a while; then she reached for my hand. I gasped. This was the first time I had physical contact with a girl. Visions of the romantic scenes in the movies and, especially Esther Williams, came over me. The girl turned and put her lips to mine. My reaction was to tighten my lips and pull back. She was insistent, kissing me fervently.

I tried to pull away because her afternoon breath reeked of the onion's I pushed her away, wiped my lips, and said, "Ugh."

She stood up with a hurt look, biting her lip, and ran away. I was a complete failure with my first romantic encounter. At that time, my awareness of onion breath had more prominence than the lure of romance.

Then there was Michael and Marco's sister Rose. She was a sweet person. Her beauty was fascinating, with her dark hair and strong Mediterranean features. When I went over to their house, Rose would try to engage me in conversation. Each time that happened, I lost all my ability to talk. Michael would bust my chops afterward about the "cat catching" my tongue because I had a crush on his sister.

Becoming a Team

Then there was baseball. The field was the magnet that drew us together. It was there that we became the ball players of two teams that had one of the best ages in baseball, the Brooklyn Dodgers and the New York Yankees—the two teams we admired the most. The legends that played on these teams are still revered to this day. Some of the names: Robinson, Reese, Erskin, Snyder, Campanella, and Furillo on the Dodgers and Mantle, and DiMaggio, Berra, MacDougald, Rizzuto, Martin for the Yankees.

I wish that there was a tape recording of the seriousness of our conversations about these baseball players that we idolized as gods. Our strong opinions about them often caused arguments with one another, sometimes almost to the point of exchanging blows. We were split evenly between Brooklyn Dodgers and New York Yankees fans.

One such conversation was about Roy Campanella. He was a great catcher for the Brooklyn Dodgers. He was often compared to Yogi Berra. I loved Roy Campanella. He was my baseball hero. He was like a brick wall at home plate. Anyone sliding into him walked away with internal injuries. I used to get in the face of Bobby Sollazzo, and we would argue over who was the better catcher Roy Campanella or Yogi Berra. Sometimes it was so heated that our fists were clenched, chest pushing one another.

> *History shows that Roy Campanella had a better batting average. Both were great players.*

Toward the end of summer, with the pennant races getting tighter, we would play softball or hardball. The grass field in August and September was a mixture of green and brown grass. The dirt base lines and the pitcher's mound were irregular shapes. A far cry from the well-manicured baseball park fields. Our equipment consisted of gloves, their leather cracking and the web held together with brown shoestring.

Baseballs, their cowhides worn from so many games, were covered with black friction tape to prevent them from falling apart. Bats that were cracked were also wrapped with friction tape to hold them together. The bases were pieces of cardboard held down by a rock to prevent them from blowing away.

To play a game, we needed eighteen players. Since there were only six of us, we had to draw on six other boys in the neighborhood— still leaving us six players short. To compensate for the missing players, each team was positioned with the first basemen playing wide from first base to handle any balls between first and second. The short stop would handle any balls between short and third and cover balls close to the left side of second base. The left and right fielders would play halfway between their fields and center to cover any balls going toward center field.

Playing with six players short was manageable. The balls we were using had layer after layer of friction tape. The friction tape added weight to the ball. When you hit the ball, it rolled slower, enabling the runner to beat the throw. The ball rarely went past the infielders. The outfielders were waving away mayflies, those gnats that clustered in fields.

The excitement of the game was paramount to us. Not playing by the rules did result in a major injury to Marco. He was the catcher, but he had no protection equipment. One game when my brother Johnny was the batter, with two runners on first and second base, he hit a line drive to centerfield. In his excitement, he threw the bat behind him. The bat went crashing into Marco's face. Marco grabbed his mouth, rolling over. His mouth was bleeding profusely. Fortunately, he did not lose any teeth, and his mouth recovered.

The following week, we got a pleasant surprise. One afternoon just as we were about to start a game, Mr. Sollazzo parked his car nearby. He called out to us, "Boys come over here," waving us to the back of his car. He had heard about Marco getting a loose bat to the mouth, almost breaking his teeth.

Opening the trunk of his car, Mr. Sollazzo started to hand out gloves, a new hardball, bats, and a catcher's equipment. "Here." That's all he said. He smiled and walked away. He did this gift because he knew we played with nothing though our hearts were into everything about the game.

One summer, he made arrangements for us to see the New York Yankees play against the Cleveland Indians at Yankee Stadium. I wasn't a Yankee fan, but going to Yankee Stadium and watching the legends of the Yankees play was exhilarating. I remember when Larry Doby of the Cleveland Indians hit a line drive. the echo of the ball hitting the bat made us shift our heads to center field as Joe DiMaggio ran and caught the ball. Little did I know at the time that I was observing the most honored center fielder in baseball history, Joe DiMaggio and also Larry Doby, the second black player to break the color barrier. Thanks to Mr. Sollazzo, we had that opportunity.

My love of baseball knew no boundaries. Whenever I could play, I would. Another time I had the opportunity to see the Brooklyn Dodgers play the Cincinnati Reds at Ebbets Field. My Uncle Jack came to visit us. Little did I know that at one time is he was a "Hawker" selling food and drink to the fans in his younger days at Ebbets Field. It was a Sunday. After we finished breakfast, he said to my mother, "Rose, don't worry about lunch. Anthony and I are going to go to a special place."

As he drove the car, I asked him what the special place was. He just smiled. Since we left our town and now the larger buildings and congestion of the city became more apparent, I had no idea of where we were headed. Then a sign with the word "Brooklyn" appeared. That was the home of my favorite baseball team.

I turned to Uncle Jack. "Why are we in Brooklyn?"

Then I saw the reason. In front of me was the stadium, and in top floor in the center of the stadium   were giant-sized letters "Ebbets Field". I thought that maybe, just maybe Uncle Jack was taking me to see the Dodgers.

Before I could ask him, he parked the car and announced "Anthony, today we are going to see the Dodgers play the Cincinnati Reds."

I was ecstatic. My dream to see the real Dodgers in action was coming to a reality before my eyes.

Uncle Jack held my hand as we went to the ticket counter inside the stadium. The boisterous crowds of Dodger fans were exchanging con-versations about the coming game. Fat guys who were smoking cigars, waited for their tickets; hardly any women were in the line. When we entered the stadium, I craned my neck following the huge steel col-umns that held up the stands. Then we walked the ramp to the second level. When we came to the exit opening to the second level, I just stood there. In front of me was the baseball field. Its lush green grass filled with players. Written across their uniform chest was the team's name—Dodgers.

All the Dodger greats. This meant more to me than the Yankee game because these were the players I idolized.

> I didn't know what Uncle Jack thought as I stood there. But I know now as I think back to that time. It most have been a wonderful sight to see a 10-year-old boy's taking in the great-ness of his idols and a dream come true.

TWELVE

"MRS. BISCEGLIA, I BROKE MY NUTS!"

Summer soon passed. We had to go back to school after Labor Day.

There were no school buses in those days. Our routine was to meet in the morning at Frank and Bobby's apartment building on Purdy Street. From there we walked the rest of the way to Halstead Avenue School. The exterior of the school is built with beautiful granite block construction with a series of distinctive Tudor-like peaks. It looked like it could have been on an English estate.

With summer over, we prolonged the walk to school, barely getting there before classes started. After experiencing the freedom that summer made, we were restless being confined to a classroom from nine in the morning to three in the afternoon. The classrooms had huge single pane windows. Some of them faced the main thoroughfare, Halstead Avenue. I always liked to sit next to the window. The first fall days of school, when the teacher left the window open a crack, I would enjoy the fresh air breeze. It gave me ample opportunity to gaze outside and watch the birds fly from tree to tree and look out at the cars and trucks on Halstead Avenue. My heart was not in the classroom; it was outside with the birds. I would daydream and imagined myself having wings and being able go wherever I wanted. When I turned away from the window, I'd look up at the Roman numeral clock, hoping it would move faster to lunch time and then later to dismissal. It seemed the minute hand was stuck in the same place. Interestingly, doing that was an education. I used to challenge myself to determine when buildings were built that had the construction date carved into the corner stone in Roman numerals. Michael and I used to argue over the date trying to prove who knew more. After school when classes were finished, we all met on the way home. All we would talk about was hanging around the fort and the forthcoming World Series. We had little interest in school compared to the freedom of fort life where we were unsupervised and planned adventurous pursuits.

Separate from our daytime classes, another part of our education was religious instructions. Every Wednesday we had to go to the *Roman Catholic Religious Instruction* class. It was held after school in the Veterans Memorial building across the street from the school. We would say that the nuns came from Heaven to teach us the *Baltimore Catechism*. Johnny, my brother, was impressed with one lesson given in religious instruction: The Catholic Church's right to make church laws and the infallibility of the Pope. The nun was citing what happened in history when the dictates of the Roman Catholic Church were not obeyed. She cited the excommunication of Martin Luther from the Roman Catholic Church when he posted *The Ninety Five Thesis* on the door of the church and also when the Pope created the Great Crusades to thwart Muslin influence on Western Civilization. The ironic part of having class there was that, after we left class, we would go to the front of the building, where two fifty-caliber dummy machine guns were set up on tripods and play war.

The nun was merely citing history. But that lesson on Martin Luther and the Great Crusades inadvertently fueled Johnny's self-righteous attitude toward others who were not Catholic. One weekend in early

October, when we were hanging around in the fort, Johnny told us stories about the Crusaders, and others like Ivanhoe and Robin Hood. He had great admiration for them. He felt that they fought for the poor and oppressed. He felt that the Crusaders, the Pope's army, were sent to rid the world of the evil tyrants in the Middle East and that the Pope's action against Martin Luther still needed to be enforced. He had a plan to pick up the mantle of the Crusaders and enforce the Pope's teachings against those who go against him—even counting the Protestants.

Johnny was clearly telling us that he felt any religion that didn't follow the Pope was evil. Oh crap, I thought. He has something up his sleeve. He always positioned his ulterior motive by stirring up your emotions.

My brother started to talk about his idea. "Pull up a crate and sit down. Look, this is how we're gonna teach those Boy Scouts at the Presbyterian Church a lesson, and this is how we are going to do it."

The Presbyterian Church was located on Harrison and Park Avenues and held the monthly Boy Scout and Cub Scout meetings in the basement of the church.

I asked, "What the heck are you talking about? I know some of those guys in that church. Michael and I are in the Cub Scout troop and go there the same night as the Boy Scouts. Why do they need a lesson?"

Johnny said, "Because it's our duty. Don't you remember what we learned in catechism class?" Johnny went into a tirade about all the injustices to the poor. He was very convincing, using our own insecurities to mount a war against the Boy Scouts meeting at the church because most of them were Protestants, privileged, and came from rich families. Then the true motive came out. He wanted revenge on the Troop because they expelled him when he and another Scout got in a fight at one meeting. He was so hurt when they expelled him from the troop that he harbored that anger, waiting for the opportune time to get back at them. I'm sure he felt that they provoked him to get him kicked out of the troop because he was not one of them in social status.

We were a gang, and he deserved our loyalty.

The plan was that Michael and I would go to our Cub Scout meeting and, when the meeting was over, we would be the first ones out of the church. Then we would signal to the rest of the gang that the meeting was over by yelling *Ringalevio*. That would let the gang know that the rest of the Scouts would be coming out soon. The gang would be hiding on the hill across the street, armed with marble-sized stones. As the rest of the Scouts walked closer to the street curb, the gang would launch the stones. After the attack, everyone was to run back into the fort.

We all sat there with our mouths open.

"You want us to wage war on the Scouts? If we get caught, we can go to jail."

Johnny said, "OK. Let's take a vote on it. Frank, make up some sticks, long and short. The long ones should be the size of the middle finger, and the short ones the size of the pinky. The long ones will be for *not* doing it, and the short ones for doing it. Give one of each to everyone. I'll hold the empty can. You can drop your stick into it. I'll be blindfolded so I won't see how you voted. OK?"

After Frank distributed the required sticks, each of us walked up to Johnny and dropped one stick into the can.

He counted the sticks. The count—four short and two long.

Some of us just shook our heads in disbelief, but "gang loyalty" was strong, so we went along with the plan. The decision to go to war with the Scouts weighed on each of us. An air of tension was felt. The fort became so quiet that a pin dropping could be heard.

By their silence John sensed that everyone was having second thoughts. Creating a distraction, he motioned with his hand toward the door for them to go outside and play war games.

We marched up Purdy Street, heading toward the train station. I started singing the Marine's Hymn that I learned from watching John Wayne in the movie *Iwo Jima*. "From the Halls of Montezuma to the shores of Tripoli. We will fight our country's battles on the land and on the sea...."

The excitement started building with the march. Then Michael yelled, "Let's go to the monuments in the park and play war!"

"Yeah," the gang shouted in unison, and everyone joined in with singing the Marine's Hymn all the way to the park. Bystanders were smiling as we walked by, saluting us as if we were real Marines.

As we approached the station, we planned our war game.

I said, "Some of us can be pilots and make like we're flying P-38's shooting at Jap Zeros. We can use the prop at the Amelia Earhart memorial as our plane."

The Amelia Earhart memorial is a bronze replica of the Lockheed 10E Electra prop plane imbedded in the stone.

Johnny was delighted that everyone had a change in mood. Wanting to keep the gang excited and on a war footing was his goal; he issued commands like a real officer. "Anthony, Michael, and Bobby! Attention!"

"Yes, Sir!" we replied.

"The three of you will go to the Amelia Earhart monument. Michael, you will sit on top of the stone, with Anthony and Bobby on each side. Michael will be the pilot, and you two will be the gunners. And the rest of us will go to the WWI soldier monument."

This memorial is a bronze lifelike statue of a soldier with his right arm raised, grenade in hand and a rifle with a bayonet held at his left side. We made believe that we were charging the enemy pill boxes with the bronze soldier. Two of us behind the soldier and the other two behind the machine guns on each side of him. We relished the thought of mowing down the enemy.

"OK, let's get going. We have a war to win!"

Michael, Bobby, and I ran off to the Amelia Earhart monument. The monument was barely discernable from the street and sidewalk, almost covered by the branches from a large pine tree. The three of us took up our positions. The cars passing the memorial would be Japanese Zeros. The people walking were soldiers.

The first car came toward the bend in the road. Michael yelled, "Japanese Zero. Rat-a-tat," mimicking a machine gun.

"We got that SOB. He's going down in a trail of smoke!" Michael shouted.

Then a train pulled into the station. We waited. Hidden by the tree branches, the passengers getting off the train and walking to their parked cars could not see us. Once they got close to us, we yelled, "Enemy troops on the road! Open fire! Rat-a-tat!" repeating the sound of the machine gun. The passengers, jolted by this sudden noise, jumped.

This went on with each pedestrian until one man got really mad after dropping his briefcase in fright and yelled, "You crazy kids scared the hell out of me. You better get out of there and stop frightening people, or I'm going to call the cops. I live across the street. So, you better not hang around. Now get the hell out of here!" With his arms folded, he stood waiting for us to leave which we reluctantly did.

We went back to join the gang at the war memorial. My brother, taking this war game seriously, demanded, "Why the hell aren't you shooting at Japanese planes?"

I explained, "Some guy who lives across the street from the station got mad at us. He said, if we didn't stop, he was going to call the cops, so we ran before he could call them."

Johnny told us the battle plan. The monument soldier was leading the charge. When Johnny said to charge, one of us would grab the rifle and pretend to be charging with him. The others would be on the machine guns at each side of the soldier, shooting at the enemy.

Michael would be feeding machine gun ammunition to the gunner who would be Frank or Marco. I had to climb up the tree behind the soldier and be an anti-aircraft gunner firing at Japanese Zeros. My brother cautioned me "not to fall out of the tree like you did a couple of years ago," and with a smile, adding a phrase that only he and I would understand, "One I feel. and one I do not feel." Although the gang would remember that fall, thankfully, they didn't know what happened after it.

Johnny was referring to a time when I was eight years old. We were all playing in the open field by the Bisceglia house, wrestling in the foot-high grass. Michael and I broke away and climbed the apple tree in the lot next to his house. That tree had to be about twenty-feet high. When I got to top of the tree, I stretched to reach the last branch and slipped, falling straight down and landing on a branch below between my legs. The scream was epic, as I rolled down to the ground clutching my testicles, tears streaming and the pain unrelenting.

Mrs. Bisceglia had come running out. "*Oh io gesu christo!* What happened Anthony?"

Choking, I felt like my guts were going to spill. "Mrs. Bisceglia, I broke my nuts!"

Eliciting a smile from her, she rushed into the house and brought a washcloth with ice cubes. "Anthony, hold this washcloth against them and go home to your mother. Michael will walk you home. Take your time and walk slowly. Capisci?"

That year I went for a hernia operation. On the day before the surgery, I went to the hospital. The nurses came into my room and put me in a wheelchair to take me for a pre-surgery examination by a doctor. They wheeled me out of the hospital room, my mother and brother Johnny there with me, and left us in a corridor to wait for the doctor.

A young intern from Poland, who spoke broken English, was to evaluate the severity of my hernia. As he approached me, I did not think this was going to be good moment for me. He was sloppy-looking, and his white coat had coffee stains. He looked like he just got out of bed. He had a dark beard shadow and his sandy hair was poorly combed. He looked dumpy, reminding me of Humpty Dumpty. The doctor directed me with a growling voice to stand up and drop my pajamas.

I thought, "Jesus, the whole world is going to look at my nuts! I don't like this guy!"

My mother was aghast since there were nurses around and others passing through the corridor. "Doctor, can't we do this someplace else?" She was trying to save me the humiliation.

"No! I have to be somewhere else. Let's take a look! Now drop your pajamas!" which I did, cupping my hands over my privates only to have him pull them away.

He reached under and felt my testicles in full view of the hospital population and exclaimed, "One I feel, and one I do not feel! I will let Dr. Sisco (the surgeon) know," and he walked away.

Mom just stood there, really ticked off.

All I could think of was "what an asshole" to tell us what we already knew.

My brother Johnny could not stop laughing. When we went back into the room he kept pinching my cheek and repeating, "One I feel and one I do not feel!"

The memory of the pain and the humiliation of that old injury made me determined to play it safe this time.

For the next couple of hours, Johnny had us do an imaginary attack, shooting and jumping over park benches as if they were pillboxes and lobbing pine-cones as hand grenades.

Hot from our exertions, we decided to bike to the Purchase, an exclusive residential area, filled with mansions and large estates. To get there, we used sidewalks that ran alongside the major artery and some of the quieter side streets that ran through Purchase. We stopped on one of those side streets just to get a rest. I looked around to see if everyone felt the same and stopped when I got to my brother Johnny. He had that smile—the one he had when there was something up his sleeve. Oh, crap here we go again, I thought.

"We're all sweaty. I have an idea," Johnny said, followed by a groan from all of us. "We can go to the reservoir, or we can sneak into one of the rich people's yards and jump into their pool without them ever seeing us. One of the houses we passed today looked like no one is home."

I challenged Johnny. "They must have someone watching their homes. Besides, we don't have any bathing suits. What are we supposed to do—swim bare ass?"

He gave me that look of betrayal. "Yeah! We're gonna swim bare ass. What's the matter? Are you chicken?"

There it was again, the magic word that turns reason into blind submission. The rest of the gang waited for a response from me that never came.

Ultimately, we decided to go. We weren't afraid of anything. After all, we were not chicken. But if someone was there, we would be in a lot of trouble.

When we cut through one of the side streets, we saw a mansion that absolutely looked like there was no one home. We could see the pool house and the pool which still had water in it. The plan was to put our bikes in the bushes across the street, and two of us would scout the property to be sure that we were right that no one was home and to determine the best way in.

We got to the mansion and slowly crept up to the wrought iron fence surrounding the estate and gathered in one spot. Johnny instructed Michael and Marco to check out the end of the fence to see if there was an opening. Marco was to follow the bushes along the driveway and get close to the house to see if anyone was home. Johnny told Marco, "Run as if a ghost from the cemetery next to the fort just came to life and was after you. Yell as loud as you can. If there are dogs, yell, 'Dogs, Dogs;' if there are people, yell, 'Owners,' and we will all get on our bikes and ride out of here as fast as we can!"

When Marco and Michael returned, Michael reported first that there was no hole in the fence. The only way we could get to the grounds was to go over the fence. And the only way we could do that was to climb one of the oak trees and jump from one of the branches hanging over the fence. The branches were pretty high. We could get hurt.

Then Marco gave his report. He went from bush to bush dodging in between them. The bushes were high, so no one could see us. He didn't hear any dogs. But when he did get close to the house, there was a light coming through the window on the front door, so he wasn't for sure if someone was home or not.

Johnny pulled away from the gang and sat down thinking about our next move. He decided that the best way was to go through the driveway. Going from bush to bush. Marco would lead since he knew the way.

One by one, we went up the driveway, dodging between the bushes until we reached the pool. We stripped down there and dove in. The water felt like a soft blanket, soothing the muscles of a long day of running and biking. We were quiet at first. But, thinking no one was home, we started to yell with each dive, splashing each other and laughing.

Suddenly, the pool spotlights came on, and a deep voice yelled from loudspeakers, "What are you doing in my pool? You little ingrates, get out, or I'll send my dogs after you! The police are on their way. You better move your little asses." This was followed by a roaring evil laugh.

The dogs never came; it was a bluff. But we thought he may have kept them quiet to see what we were up to while we were scouting the property.

Johnny yelled to everybody, "Pick up your clothes and run. We have to get out of here before the cops come. There's no time to change. Hurry!"

I wish that I had a photo of that Moment. There we were, the Purdy Street Gang, some bare-assed and some with clinging underwear, running down the driveway of a large estate, fumbling with our clothes, fearful that any moment a dog would bite us.

We ran to the bushes where our bikes had been hidden. Unfortunately for some of us, we jumped into briar bushes which scratched our legs, arms, and butts. Hurriedly we put on our clothes, fighting time, worried the police were on their way. With no time to put on our shoes and socks, we tied the shoes with the socks looped over our handlebars, jumped on our bikes riding faster—it seemed—than the cars on the major road to town.

When we got to our neighborhood, it was well past suppertime. We looked like hell. Scratches on our bodies from the bushes. Feet dirty from riding without shoes. Our day of war ended with a humiliating defeat at the pool.

I asked, nervously, "What do we tell Mom when we get home?"

Johnny chuckled and said, "We'll say that we were playing with the Marco and Michael and that they threw us into the hedges." He always had an answer.

THIRTEEN

"RINGOLEVIO"

The daring mischievous adventures of summer were minor compared to that October night of the joint Boy Scout and Cub Scout meeting. When I came home from school that afternoon before the meeting, my mother had a pot of gravy cooking on the stove with a loaf of Italian bread on a dish. It was macaroni night. The aroma of the gravy lured me to the pot, my mouth watering in anticipation of the flavors of meat, tomatoes, olive oil, and spices. I ripped off a piece of Italian bread and dunked it into the sauce.

Mom was standing bent over the ironing board, pressing my blue Cub Scout uniform, watching me out of the corner of her eye. She smiled as I dipped the bread. Because I was anxious to see the uniform, I approached her while, in my hand, was a piece of Italian bread drenched in gravy and leaving a trail behind. Mom dropped the iron and smiled, but with a sharp command. "Stop!"

I didn't move a step further until I finished the bread. Mom would have been furious if the gravy droppings touched the uniform.

She purchased the regulation Cub Scout shirt from a uniform store, but she had limited funds and could not afford the regulation pants, so she made the pants with their golden yellow ribbing on the pockets. She was an accomplished seamstress. But the homemade pants were a shade lighter than the Cub Scout blue, resulting in a slight contrast.

Disappointed in the contrast, I made an ungrateful comment, "Mom, the pants look lighter than the shirt. I don't want to go to the meeting looking like this. The pants don't look like the real Cub Scout pants."

She put the iron down and just stared at me, with one hand holding the iron. Her eyes welled, and I thought for sure she was going to cry. It had taken her a couple of weeks to get the material and make those pants. Surely, she thought it would make me happy. My comment was a disappointment and angrily she said, "Anthony, I could only afford the shirt. The pants are not that different in color. And no one will notice or care. You are going to the meeting. Be happy with what you have!"

I started to object, but Sonny, my older brother, overheard the conversation and held up his right hand like a traffic officer, lips tightened with the other hand on his side making a fist signaling a punch. I could tell he was angry. It was enough of a warning for me to be silent and say no more.

When the uniform was ironed, it looked like a military-style one with sharp creases.

Mom was particularly careful with the yellow scarf, making sure it was creaseless. That night, as I put my pants and shirt on, I grabbed the Cub Scout Neckerchief and looped it around my neck, grasping each end to pull it through the scarf holder.

My mother came over to check my appearance and said, "Now, let's make sure you look neat and sharp for your meeting." She rearranged the scarf ends, smiling as she did it, making sure the pointed angle of the scarf, with the wolf and logo, was centered on my back.

She noticed I was nervous and said, "Anthony, what's the matter? Don't worry. You'll be fine tonight." For Michael and me, it was going to be the night we would take our first step toward becoming Boy Scouts. My mother was also looking forward to it

It wasn't the meeting I was nervous about; it was the torment I felt inside. I was going to meet with my fellow Scouts and, unbeknownst to them, I was plotting with my brother and the gang to do harm to them. Deep inside me, I wanted so much to be a part of the troop. I knew that what we were about to do would likely prevent that from ever happening.

When Johnny came into the room, Mom turned to me and said, "Your brother is going to take you and Michael to the meeting and wait to take you home when it ends. Make sure you come home with him."

"Ok, Mom. I will."

Johnny looked into my eyes and held his finger up to his lips. "*Shh*," when I almost blurted out the devious plan we were about to launch. He and I left the house about 6:30 p.m. to head to the meeting room in the church basement. We picked up Michael along the way. As we walked toward the church, Johnny stopped. "Now listen, you two. Remember the plan. After your Scout meeting, make sure you're the first ones out. The sidewalk with the hedges on each side will force you into a line of two abreast. I need to know you're clear of the group, so yell, '*Ringolevio*' and dash across Park Avenue, head to the hill behind the fort, and stand with us. We're gonna teach those Protestants and rich kids a lesson! Once you're safe with us, the gang is gonna send a barrage of stones at them and watch the cowards run. We will be victorious!"

The whole time we were walking with him, Michael and I didn't know what to say. The October night was so serene—a full moon with brilliant star clusters. Normally I would be looking at them and whistling and Michael and I would be talking the whole time. But that night, I looked at Michael. We were afraid that if we didn't do what Johnny wanted, he would cold shoulder us for betraying him, and we did not know what else he would do.

> When my Mom passed away years later, Michael came up to me. Not seeing Johnny and I for many years, he pulled me aside. "Anthony, is that Johnny?" He did not recognize my brother. "You know, Anthony, he use to scare the shit out of me. Remember the night of the Cub Scout meeting and the battle. I wanted to run away from him but was too scared." We both smiled in agreement.

Finally, at the church hall, we went inside to the meeting. The Scouts all stood at attention. The meeting began with the Scout Pledge and Scout Law. As I repeated the pledge, a sense of remorse came over me. I would soon violate both.

As they always did at every meeting, the Scoutmasters were reiterating the importance of duty, honor, and loyalty to country, and respect for others.

After the pledge and the Scoutmaster's words, Michael and I were wavering and maybe we would pull out of Johnny's plan . What were we to do? Was betrayal of one's friends more of a mortal sin than adhering to the principals of the Scout Code? Michael and I understood that the bond of friendship meant more than siding with people outside of the gang. It might be wrong, but we had to see the plan through even if it meant going against our feelings.

The meeting ended. As we were about to leave, the Scoutmaster came up to us encouraging us to join the Boy Scouts.

We said nothing, but we bowed our heads. The Scoutmaster had a quizzical look on his face as he saw our response. Before we turned toward the door, I looked up once again at the Scoutmaster and stared at him for a moment, wondering what he would think of us after tonight's assault by the gang.

Then we left.

Michael and I raced to the head of the line and out the door. When we reached the street, the line of Scouts, walking two by two, were just getting to the end of the hedges. We looked right and left for cars. Then we ran across Park Avenue, yelling "*Ringolevio*," the signal that we were clear of the troop.

As we got to the edge of the woods and out of sight, a barrage of rocks came through the night sky. Stone after stone hit the Scouts. They cried out in pain and were holding their hands over their heads like people trying to avoid a rainstorm, bobbing and weaving to escape the barrage. The line broke, and the Scouts scattered all over Park Avenue, some escaping and others getting hit. One Scout who was hit I think was the son of the police chief of the Town of Harrison. A stone had grazed his head and blood flowed down his left cheek. He ran five blocks up on Harrison Avenue from the church to the police station, where his father was on duty.

Watching the Scouts scatter, we roared, "Victory! Victory! Look at the cowards run!"

Laughing, we made our way up the hill to the fort. Once we were inside, we lit a campfire and pulled out some cigarettes, puffing away and resting against the fort walls with a sense of pleasure.

Johnny was elated. "Good work, men! We showed the rich Protestants who's better—the Italians of the Purdy Street Gang!"

"Yeah! Yeah!" we echoed, followed by a chorus of laughter, feeling a sense of superiority over the Protestant boys. Our feeling was that we taught them a lesson that we were better than them.

Another burst of laughter. A few more stories. More laughter.

We were feeling our oats, our imagined invincibility. We were unaware of the physical harm we had actually done to some of the Scouts. And little did we know what response was coming.

The night was so crisp and clear as we sat around on our crates smoking and blowing smoke up to the brilliant night. Suddenly there was a loud clang of the cans that we'd strung along the length of the field—our warning system—alerting us to the approach of intruders.

We dropped our cigarettes and looked apprehensively at one another. Johnny raised his arm to Marco, who was our lookout, and said in a low voice, "Marco, did you hear that? Hurry up and go to the tower and see if anyone is coming."

Marco scurried like a squirrel up the ladder, rung by rung, until he reached the tower platform. I could see him kneeling on the platform so as not to reveal his position and straining his eyes. I could see a look of disbelief on his face. He saw some silhouettes that were larger in size than the Boy Scouts but were moving slowly toward the fort. Marco shouted down to us "Shit! Those stupid Scouts are coming. And it looks like they have their big brothers with them."

We didn't know who was approaching. Fear of physical harm came over most of us with the urge to run.

Marco whispered, "Johnny, what do you want to do? There's a line of them crossing the field. They're bigger than us. We're in deep trouble! We better get the hell out of here!"

Johnny yelled up, "No! Stay put and let us know how close they get.

Everyone, go to the walls and load the slingshots. If they get any closer, wait for my command to fire. We fight!"

As the shadows got closer, my brother ran up one of the ramps, loaded a slingshot and fired a salvo of rocks at the intruders.

Suddenly, the intruders charged the fort, unaware of the moats. The ground swallowed them one by one. They had dog dung on their shoes, and the pointed punji sticks ripped their clothes.

Then we all began to unleash our slingshots.

We could hear them struggling to get out of the moats, shouting, "You wait 'til we get our hands on you, you little bastards!"

And then another yelled. "Dammit, I got dog shit all over my uniform. I'm going to kill the first one I get my hands on."

With the word "uniform" shouted, and as the intruders got closer, we turned toward each other in realization that they were the Harrison Police Department. We quickly assumed that the son of the town's police chief squealed on us and told his dad about the fort.

Their anguished roars coming from the moats reinforced our fears that we were in deep trouble. Their voices were getting closer and closer, and salvo after salvo of rocks were launched at them. We were hoping that the sling shots would deter them, but the officers finally made it to the front door.

One officer tried to break it open with his foot. He almost broke his leg because we had it wedged with two logs at a forty-five-degree angle. Finally, they broke a wall into splinters with an ax. They came rushing in with flashlights crossing back and forth.

They tried to grab whomever was closest. Johnny was caught and dragged out to a squad car. Michael, with his quick motions, eluded them and got away. Bobby and Frank got out and ran to their apartment building and hid in the cellar. As my brother tried to get away, the officer gave him a good kick in the butt. I ran to a dark corner of the fort and hid inside a nail barrel, shaking with fear, hoping to not pee in my pants. How I ever got into that small wood barrel is beyond me. To this day, I don't know how I did it.

After the police left, taking Johnny in the squad car, a deafening stillness enveloped the fort. The only sounds were the whooshing of cars on Purdy Street and Park Avenue. I was so petrified that my body wouldn't move, as I attempted to get out of the barrel. Then I heard steps outside. One of the cops had come back to make sure no one remained. Flashing his light from one corner to the other, the beam hit me. The officer held the light on me for a moment. Frozen in position, hands cupping my face and my body leaning into the wall joint, my silhouette and the barrel might have looked like a large piece of wood. He put the light down and turned to leave.

After he left, I thought I was alone as the night's stillness returned. I finally wiggled my way out of the barrel when I suddenly heard a creaking sound and the tower was swaying.

"Marco! Marco! Are you up there? Are the cops gone?"

"Anthony! Is that you?"

"Yes."

"The cops are gone. But we're gonna get our asses handed to us when we get home!" He came down from the lookout tower, and we went to where the front door once was. We peaked our heads outside, not knowing whether to go home or hide.

Finally, Marco put his arm around my shoulder I was about to cry. All

I could think of was that we went to war with the cops and that they would put us in reform school.

We were looking in every direction, anticipating and worrying that the police would come again. "Marco, do you see any cops?"

"No. Let's get the hell out of here!"

We hightailed it out of there like two deer in flight for their lives and headed for home.

FOURTEEN

"JESUS, WHAT WERE THEY THINKING?"

Marco and I ran all the way home, panting in fear and the exertion from running, looking behind us, expecting too be caught by a police officer at any moment. I was afraid the police would take us to the station house. By the time I got home, my forehead was beaded with sweat, the droplets running through the dirt on my face. I opened the door so fast it startled my mother, causing her to drop a dish, shattering it on the floor.

"Anthony, what's the matter? Look at what you made me do!" With a troubled look and she asked, "Why are you breathing so hard? Where is your brother? What happened to you? Why are you so dirty? Did you get into a fight? What's going on?"

I stood frozen, unable to respond. Before I could answer any one of her questions, there was a knock on the door.

She thought it was my brother Johnny.

As she approached the door, she said, "Johnny, I know it's you. Stop fooling around." When she opened the door, a police officer was standing before her.

My mother turned her head toward me. She was biting her lower lip, and the look on her face said, "*What do you know about this, Anthony?*" When our eyes met, I realized that this night would cast shame on us as a family. It would fuel the evil words of the old lady across the street. She often complained to other neighbors that we were bad kids. One time she went to the county social services with her complaints. The social worker explained to Mom, if our neighbor across the street continued to make complaints, that the county would follow up with a hearing. An unfavorable ruling could result in our being taken away. Although the social worker did not threaten Mom, it was a warning that hung over her like a cloud especially when we got into trouble.

My mother invited the officer into the house, but her worried expression became even graver.

The officer explained to her that Johnny was being held at the police station. He explained why. For her son to come home, she would have to sign a release. He went on to explain the series of events and consequences of throwing rocks at the Boy Scouts, hurting several of them. One of the boys ran to the station with his head bleeding from the salvo of stones cast, and from the sling shot rock assault on the police officers almost injuring them.

My mother, in shock, her eyes welling with tears, gasping, held the back of a kitchen chair to steady herself. Three hours earlier, she was looking forward to my going to a Scout meeting, trusting Johnny with taking me. Now she had a police officer in front of her. She couldn't comprehend why Johnny was at the police station. I was worried that we would be taken away.

My mother stood there with her look of disbelief, that a boy was hurt and that we shot stones from slingshots at the officers.

Her response to the officer was—"Jesus, what were they thinking?"

Mom turned toward me with a look of betrayal, her eyes narrowed, and her fists clenched. She grabbed my hand so tight that it felt like the bones were being crushed as she took me with her to the police car

The drive to the station house was silent. The only sounds inside the car were the shifting gears and the two-way radio. I was in the back seat of the patrol car with Mom, both of us looking straight ahead. Avoiding any eye contact with her, I focused on the front windshield.

When she got out of the car, my mother stood for a moment and looked at the station house, containing her anger, grabbing my hand and pulling me as she walked into the station and up to the front desk. Mom and the officer sat me down on a bench in front of the desk. They disappeared down the hall. I had no idea where they were going or where my brother was.

Alone on that bench, I felt uneasy. I was alone. None of my friends were there. Was something going to happen to me? I had visions of Johnny's arms dangling from a chain and the police torturing him, lashing a whip across his back. Each time an officer walked past me, I would look up at their stern faces that conveyed the seriousness of what we had done.

Then Mom came walking toward me with my brother Johnny. I felt a sense of relief that I was not going to be punished or put away. She approached the night desk officer who handed her a paper to sign and who released Johnny into her custody.

My mother, with an irate voice, said, "Let's go home." Then turning to the officers, she apologized for what happened, expressing her concern that the Scouts or police officers were hurt.

Grabbing each of us by the hand, we left the. police station, Mom with her head bowed signifying her humiliation. Johnny's and my hands were in pain from her crushing grip as she yanked us outside.

Once outside, she let go and set a fast pace as we walked home behind her. She was bristling. Every so often, she turned her head toward us. "Why did you do this to me?" she asked as she looked up toward the evening sky with a look of uncertainty of what was to follow after that night.

Johnny had a worried look on his face. He turned to me and told me about his time in the jail cell. The cell was dirty, the colors of the wall were a deep worn yellow. The toilet bowl was filthy. It was not pleasant. In the couple of hours, he spent there, he started to think that he would be locked up forever. That he would lose his freedom. He said that it was the worse feeling he ever had.

As he told me this, all I could think of was the old lady across the street and what the county worker told Mom. Was this what would happen to us after tonight?

When we got home and inside, Mom turned around and with tears in her eyes, said, "How could the two of you do this to us? Ruin our family name? Hurt all those boys and the police? How dare you do this?" She slammed her fist to the table so hard the salt and pepper shakers fell popped up in the air and fell off the table.

She then proceeded to do the one thing she rarely did, whack the living hell out of both of us. The sting of her slap across my face sent shock waves, like church bells ringing, my ears, vibrating like a tuning fork. And my butt hurt so much that lying flat on my back was not an option that night. I went to bed feeling that I had betrayed my mother, the other Boy Scouts, and myself. Sure, we all thought it was fun. But little did we know how much damage it had caused. It was that Mom's anger made me realize how harmful and hurtful what we did was to others. It was then with Moms anger that I realized how harmful and hurtful what we did to others. It brought back the horrific memories with the twin brothers when they stabbed and slashed my face with an ice pick.

The next day, Johnny and I picked up the other boys on our way to school. As we did every day, we compared notes on what had happened to each other after we all got home. I don't think any one of us escaped getting our butts handed to us. Although some of the others escaped, the news reached their parents, too.

That day in school was also revealing. Perhaps the word was all over town. Fellow students avoided Johnny and me. It was like we had some kind of disease.

Maybe I was self-conscious, but I thought that my teacher cast a wary eye, guarding against any influence I might have on other classmates. Each time I moved in my seat; the teacher gave me a sharp condescending look. I couldn't wait for the day to end. I watched the hands of the wall clock move slowly over the Roman numerals while I hoped the hands would soon indicate 3 p.m.

The gang met after school as usual to walk home. We talked and nervously laughed about the night before, images of the cops stumbling into the moats and the Scouts running in all directions. The fear I had the night before with being caught and Mom's reaction were beginning to wear off. We continued toward the fort with our normal walk routine on the way home from school. As we approached Colonial Street, we saw a dark plume of smoke billowing into the sky from the wooded area behind the field. When we got to the crest of the street, we saw some people gawking at the wooded area.

We looked at one another.

Johnny said, "Shit, the smoke is coming from the fort's location. Hurry, let's run!"

Guessing the worst, we pushed our way through the spectators. Once we got through, we gasped! Our assumption was correct. The fort was gone, and the lookout tower nothing but a scarred burnt stump.

The fire was no accident. The town planned its destruction while we were in school. They eradicated it with a controlled burn by the fire department. We later heard that, anticipating that we might show up, the police cordoned the area to prevent anyone, especially us, from trying to save the burning fort. They were determined to destroy every bit of it.

We could do nothing but look at the smoldering ruins. My brother Johnny's lips quivered as he watched. His dream fort was annihilated.

Totally demoralized, we walked away, hands in pockets, heads bowed. All our work to build the fort was obliterated.

We arrived at Frank and Bobby's apartment building and sat on the front steps, not saying a word. We felt betrayed. The town had kept us in the dark, knowing that the cops and fire department would burn the fort down, making sure we would not be there to try to stop them.

The feeling of betrayal settled as we sat there unable to comprehend why they burnt the fort down. I looked toward my brother Johnny. He just kept on staring at the billowing smoke, totally absorbed with it. I knew he was hurt. The rest of the guys telegraphed their feelings, some with clenched fists, others by pacing. We just did not know how to handle this setback.

We were furious. But it was over, never to be again. The cops were sending us a message for our own good, although we didn't think so at that instant. It was the first time in our lives that we felt the loss of something we had worked so hard for. We turned toward each other, angry, biting our lips and trying so hard to be brave. In the stillness of that moment, we all felt alone and vulnerable, a quiet realization that by being reckless we had destroyed the very thing that made us happy.

It took away our innocence. A child's freedom knows no boundaries, but the realistic limitations of the adult world had been impressed upon us.

My brother Johnny, with revenge on his mind, startled us back to the Moment. "They destroyed our fort! Now they'll have to pay for it!"

Flabbergasted, we all asked, "Johnny, what the hell are you talking about? Are you nuts? They'll put us all away if we do anything crazy."

"Look, we had money buried in the ground. That money is gone. Burned. And it cost us money to build the fort, too. With the money we lost and the materials we bought, we lost about seventeen dollars total. And I plan on getting it back from the town."

We thought for sure he was losing his mind. He wanted us to go to the police station and ask for the money. I was thinking the only thing they'll give us a swift kick in the ass for sure or put us in a cell again. No way was I gonna ask them for any money.

Johnny persisted, "Look, we worked hard on the fort. I know we screwed up, but that didn't give them the right to burn it down. Let's try to get something for our hard work." He went on to convince us that we should go to the Town Supervisor, Mr. Sulla, and ask for our money back from the town.

The next day after school, the six of us went to town hall. It was located in the same building as the police station. As we approached the hallway, the desk sergeant and the other officers saw us. We told them we were there to see the Town Supervisor and then quickly ran up the stairs to the supervisor's office and plopped our butts down on the chairs in the reception area.

Supervisor Sulla, hearing the commotion, came out of his office. He stood there looking at us with a perplexed look. His secretary hunched her shoulders signaling: *I don't know what they want.*

Everyone turned toward Johnny. "Mr. Sulla, we know we did wrong. For that, we're sorry. Very sorry. My mother made it so that we would never forget how sorry we are. But, Mr. Sulla, we put a lot of time and effort into building that fort. It was our home away from home. It cost us seventeen dollars in materials. The police were right to be angry with us for what we did. But it didn't give them the right to burn down our fort."

Everyone was silent. We were looking at one another.

Mr. Sulla had a look of disbelief. He was tapping a pencil, weighing how to respond. I think he was in awe and impressed at the set of balls this kid Johnny and his gang had. But he was also impressed with the unity of the gang. With pencil in hand, he asked us to make a list of each item that made up the seventeen dollars, explaining that it was needed for him to submit to the town so that we could get paid.

Johnny wanted the money now. "Mr. Sulla, I have the list already prepared for you." He handed it to the supervisor on written on a piece of brown paper from a supermarket bag.

Mr. Sulla read over it, occasionally looking up at Johnny and then back to the list.

Johnny was squirming a bit trying to anticipate what questions Mr. Sulla might have. If he felt the junk we collected was not worth anything, he would tell us to get lost and that the list wasn't worth a dime.

Then Mr. Sulla put forth the question that Johnny feared. "Do you have receipts for these items?" He knew that we didn't.

Silence. Johnny's eyes rolled to the ceiling.

Mr. Sulla probably knew that few things were actually purchased, yet he agreed to give us the seventeen dollars. But he also let us know he wasn't pleased about what happened and that he expected us not to do anything like that again. With that agreement, he reached into his pocket and pulled out his wallet and handed Johnny seventeen dollars.

The nervousness we felt before going to meet Mr. Sulla disappeared with smiles as we watched him hand the money to Johnny. After thanking him, we raced outside, excited about the reimbursement and crowding around Johnny pestering him to let us see the money.

None of us ever had that much money in our possession. Johnny held the money, fanning the bills like a poker player's hand. The bills included portraits of George Washington and Ben Franklin, their stoic faces a contrast to the jubilant smiles of the gang. Johnny went next door to the candy store, which was a mistake. He had the Ben Franklin bills converted to singles to distribute the money to everyone in the gang.

When Johnny handed me my portion, I grasped the dollar bills and folded them several times. I was in disbelief that dollar bills were in my possession and that one dollar bill represented a hundred pennies collected for beer and soda bottles. What an exuberant feeling it was; for the first time, I had money to buy what I wanted and won't have to scrounge for bottles. Unleashed with this newfound financial independence, I blew the first dollar buying candy, comic books, and baseball cards, saving the rest for another day.

We all had thought my brother was crazy approaching the Town Supervisor, but his persistent justification that "we were wronged," satisfied our remorseful feelings over the loss of the fort. When it came to issues right or wrong, Johnny had the unique ability to marshal unity among the gang. In this particular moment, with the destruction of the fort by the town, he showed the strong side of his leadership.

When the excitement with the money settled down, we went back to the Purdy Street Field where the fort once stood. We stood in ashes where once the front door hung. Kicking the ashes, watching them shift with the breeze, was a grim reminder of the fire that engulfed and destroyed it.

I thought how wrong it is for someone to destroy what another built with such vengeance and destruction.

Johnny was right in telling Mr. Sulla, "Yes, we did wrong, but the town had no right to destroy our fort."

A few days later in *The Daily Item*, a small headline article appeared: "Purdy Street Gang gets seventeen dollars from Town of Harrison for fort burning." It described the burning of the fort and Mr. Sula's personal contribution, which gave us a lesson in compassion as well as a stern warning.

Unfortunately, I don't know what happened to the clipping from the paper. For years, we had the article in a scrap book. Maybe Mom lost it.

FIFTEEN

"PUSH UP, PUSH UP."

My brother and I had a couple of dollars left. After parting with the gang, we decided on our way home that it would be best to give the money to Mom. We thought this for two reasons: one was that she could always use it to help with expenses, and the other was we knew that Mom was very angry and disappointed with us. We hoped that giving her the money would make her feel better about us.

But Mom's heels were dug in. No amount of money would make her feel any better about what we did the night of the Boy Scout meeting . She had a look of worry because we put her in a very uncomfortable position with the neighbors, the school, and the authorities. She had a meeting with Mr. Marshall, the principal of our school. I don't know what transpired at that meeting, but Mom was very nervous afterwards. I think it was about that night. Soon after the meeting, she warned us that people were going to watch our behaviors, and that if we got in trouble again, she would have to bend to the will of the authorities which could result in us being taken away from her. Was she actually told this? I don't know, but it was effective.

A week later, at school, Mr. Marshall stopped me in the hallway on my way to class. I was nervous, knowing that many in the adult world were unhappy with us. I thought for sure he was going to lecture me, but his reason was quite the opposite. When he approached, his radiant smile and soft manner conveyed a feeling of friendship. This particular time he had a subdued smile not his usual one. Bending toward me, he said ten words: "Anthony, if you need any help, come and see me." Then he waved me on to class.

I gave a deep sigh, releasing pent-up air.

This was not unusual behavior for him. He was that rare breed who would do anything to help a child. In fact, a few times my brother Johnny forgot his lunch. With Johnny having no money to buy lunch, Mr. Marshall would give him the money, never asking for it back or letting my mother know about his act of kindness. He was an exceptional person that only had the interest of the students at heart. I thought how good it was of him to offer me the help. How could I disappoint him from that day on?

Then there was the day I went to gym class. The physical education teacher was Mr. Fiore. My friends and I used to think that he looked like a Hollywood actor—Roman features, black hair, olive complexion, and very athletic. He also coached the high school football team. When you went to Mr. Fiore's class, you did only one thing: exercise. I thought surely that week he would be out to punish me. The lesson that particular day was to exceed our push-up number from the week before. Down we went on the floor with "Push up, push up," echoing in our ears.

When I got to thirty push-ups, I laid down on the floor. I had exceeded my push-up count by ten from the week before.

Mr. Fiore came over to me and sternly asked, "How many pushups did you do?"

I told him thirty.

"Get up. You can do more. Just try."

I felt that he wanted to punish me, and I really did not feel like doing any more push-ups, but reluctantly I did.

He stood by me and started counting "31, 32, 33..." His cadence got stronger with each word until I could do no more. When it was over, he had gotten me to sixty push-ups.

I laid flat on the floor, amazed at my number of push-ups. I was exhausted.

Mr. Fiore stood over me and, with a smile, he said, "Nice work, Anthony. You did good. Next time, we'll try for a hundred!" And he eventually did get me to one hundred push-ups.

My 4th grade teacher was a different story. When I went to class, I felt a change in her attitude—not from a learning standpoint but a personal one. You know how sometimes a kid whispers in class while cuffing the side of his mouth? I sat in the back of the classroom. When I went to whisper something to a fellow student, the teacher would stomp to the back of the classroom and stand by my desk and stare. But she would not say anything unless it interfered with the class. When we had lessons that required concentration, she would linger in the back of the room. She never did that prior to the night of the battle. Frankly, I was afraid to look up. I didn't want to look at her intense stare.

The aftermath of that night was the realization for all of us that what we thought were playful adventures had created a schism of trust between us and the adult world. Johnny and I, in particular, would be on trial more than the rest of the gang because Johnny was singled out as the "Instigator" which was unfair to him since everyone was complicit.

I became increasingly worried for my mother. When Mom went out grocery shopping, she felt a sense of shame because Johnny was put in jail, so she avoided eye contact with the neighbors. The old lady next door ramped up her poisonous condemnation of us and our mother, filling the ears of the neighbors. Our neighborhood, in particular our street Parson Street, was mostly Italian immigrants/first generation Americans. Once they fixated their opinions, we felt isolated by their murmuring and their stares. And that was what the old lady was doing.

The excitement we felt the night of the battle and receiving reparation from the town was short lived. The realization of the aftermath forced us to modify our behavior. With the fort gone and our aspirations to have a place to hang out unsupervised, we had to find better and more constructive ways to channel our energy. We had to restore the trust of our parents and town authorities, and everyone in the neighborhood and school.

What we thought are we left with now that the fort is gone? We still had the Purdy Street field and cave. The cave, we thought, would be to small and cold in the winter. That would not be a great place to hang out. We could play football on the field, and we did that almost every day after school and on the weekends until the ground became frozen.

It was the end of October. The last real big event we planned was for Halloween. We grouped that night going door to door with a pillowcase, hoping to fill it with candy. In some instances, we would run into boys from the Brentwood section resulting in confrontations. Usually they backed off because we had Frank who was so much taller

The gang had a curfew to be home by 8:30. Johnny and I stayed out later, not because we wanted more candy, but because we were hoping to receive more money. We knocked on doors until 9:30. When we got home, we dumped the entire contents of the bag on the kitchen table. Mom and Sonny helped us sort the candy and the money. That night we could not believe how much we collected. The money was more important to us. We collected about twenty dollars. Johnny and I were happy with the amount, but we knew that all we would keep that night was the candy. We both agreed that whatever money we collected would go to Mom so she could have some money for other things and expenses. "Here, Mom. You keep the money."

Her eyes closed for a brief moment, then she put her hands over them as if to cry and she gave us both a hug. "Thank you. Now we can have meatballs twice a week for a while." With a smile, she added, "But I want each of you to keep a dollar. Spend it wisely.

Johnny and I smiled with her. It felt like we repaired some of the damage to her trust.

> Comparing the Halloween bounty with the gang proved to be difficult for me. As each boasted of the candy and money collected, I felt the sting of poverty since the others could use what money they collected for whatever they wanted, while Johnny and I would need it for survival.

SIXTEEN

"I MOVED MY HANDS ACROSS THE LETTERS..."

With the fort gone. Playing outdoors on the Purdy Street field became more difficult. The fall weather was getting colder. Rain ruined the field, making football a game of mud ball. The other option was to use the town recreation center, the Aranac. From the outside, the center looked like an enormous yet ordinary two-story, with dark brown cedar-shingled home with a fieldstone foundation. The plain exterior appearance, which was not very appealing, would make one hesitate before entering. It looked tired and worn. But once inside, the excitement of boys, their jubilant or vanquished cries, as they played games reverberating throughout the center conveyed the complete opposite.

The center had a magnificent basketball court. The hardwood court floors always had a sheen. When you stood in the court and looked up at the ceiling, vaulted steel beams arched above the dark wainscoting. When I first started playing on that court, I felt something majestic was driving me to play the game. It was the court. To be on it every day moving about shooting baskets, dodging other players, rising to the game, the echoes of others that played on that court, cheered me on.

Beyond the court, there were rooms for ping pong and board games, always filled, and a bowling alley in the basement.

Then there was also the wrestling room walled off from the basketball court. The wrestling room had been a favorite place for Michael and me to kill time while we waited to use the basketball court.

We stopped using that when Michael pushed down too hard on my shoulders and broke my collar bone. He was so damn strong. After he broke my collar bone, I couldn't play basketball. I would complain to my mother that my shoulder hurt, but my brothers Johnny and Sonny thought I was faking. They took me outside and forced me to shoot baskets on a makeshift hoop on a telephone pole outside of Mark and Michael's house. I ran home crying in agony. Mom saw my pain and decided next day to take me to the doctor. He confirmed a broken collar bone. Well once we got home, my brothers caught hell from her.

The Aranac, which was open from lunch time until 9:00 p.m. every day except Sunday, became our second home. The recreation commissioner was Mr. Sollazzo, Frank and Bobby's father. He was a pillar of strength and example. Tall and muscular, dark hair, he carried his large frame with ease. He reminded me of the actor Victor Mature who played brawny roles such as in the movie *Samson and Delilah*.

Mr. Sollazzo always had a smile, especially when he approached us. It was the kind of smile that telegraphed *What are these kids up to now?* I often felt Frank and Bobby were lucky to have a father like him, reminding them often that Johnny and I wished we had one, and if we did, he would be one like Mr. Sollazzo

> Years later, the town named the center in honor of Frank P. Sollazzo . Today, the recreation center it is still named for him: The Sollazzo Center.

Mr. Sollazzo knew us better than most people in the neighborhood. He knew we were mischievous, but not bad boys. I'm sure that he wanted us off the streets as much as my mother did before we'd get hurt or into greater trouble than that night of the Boy Scout meeting. Not wanting us to get into further problems, he encouraged us to use the Aranac as a place to play basketball or just hang around.

Once we started to go to the Aranac, we couldn't get enough of the excitement and comraderies with other boys from different parts of the town. The activity we loved the most, of course, was basketball. Mr. Sollazzo knew that we spent most of our time on the court.

Some of the towns in Westchester County had junior league basketball teams. Each team would play against other teams within the county. Mr. Sollazzo knew how competitive we were and that the seeds for a cohesive team were naturally in place because of our strong brotherhood. One day, he approached us while we were playing on the court. "Boys, I'm going to form a team to represent the Aranac. I want you boys to be on that team."

I remember how he carefully surveyed each of us, looking for the eagerness and excitement in our eyes as we turned toward each other surprised, then with grateful smiles. He gave us the option of naming the team. The pro team we most admired was the NY Knickerbockers . We decided that our team name would also be the Knickerbockers. Like the school coach and principal, Mr. Marshall, Mr. Sollazzo looked to channeling our energies in a positive direction. What an honor he bestowed on us that we would be a good choice to represent the recreation commission as a basketball team playing throughout the county. It sent a message to others that the kids known as the Purdy Street Gang were abandoning their reckless nature.

When Mr. Sollazzo told us that the recreation commission would provide the uniforms, I remember jumping up. "You mean we will get real uniforms just like the professional basketball players? And we will travel to other towns?"

He went into more detail on how many games we would play and how we would have practice every day after school. But first, before we played one game, we had to learn the official game of basketball, not the street rules that we had learned while playing in the neighborhood. Those were more of a free-for-all than any semblance to the proper game. Or we played one on one. The basket we had used was a bottomed-out fruit basket nailed to a telephone pole. Our court was the street. We had very little knowledge of the real game.

I was thrilled when he told us that he was going to be our coach. To be so close to him was a privilege for Johnny and me. We felt secure that the person we respected was going to show us a better way to channel our energies.

Mr. Sollazzo could see we were excited yet apprehensive. To alleviate apprehensions and to build our confidence, he started a regimen of practice sessions. He went over everything at each practice: Instilling the rules of the game. Making us learn the strategy of each play.

The first time we turned up for practice, we thought surely that we would go to the gym and start practicing. Instead, he sat us down in one corner of the court. With a writing pad, he illustrated drawings of the basketball court at the foul line with a number from 1 to 5 indicated. Mr. Sollazzo pointed to the drawings. We were going to learn what the game of basketball was about. He stressed that we had to understand the sport, how to work as a team, and the importance of respecting and helping each other to win games.

> When I think back to that moment, I realize that he knew instinctively that we could be a very good basketball team. Teams could be good if they have strong relationships among teammates. We had that most important element: We were playmates since kindergarten. Hearing him say that we were a team had a new meaning to me since I always thought of us

as a family of brothers. In that session, Mr. Sollazzo helped us understand the importance of the word teammate.

He went over the positions of each player that first practice and then at each practice after that until we became a cohesive unit, emphasizing that every game involves knowing the assigned position and its importance.

The numbers on his pad suddenly came to life with his explanation of each of those positions:

"The number 1 position is the *point guard, the ball handler*, and *passer*. The number 2 position is the shooting guard who will position himself during the game to drive the ball to the basket or to shoot from a vantage point."

Wow, I thought, Michael and I could be in those positions. We were the fastest. And I knew that we could handle the ball better than the others. We always outwitted them with our quick moves when we played on the street.

"The number 3 position," Mr. Sollazzo said, "is the *forward* who moves around like a shooting guard but perform more moves—going in for layups and moving about the basket, drawing in the opponent sometimes to foul them, offering an opportunity to get a point on the foul line."

Michael and I could play this position, too. But maybe Marco would be better in this. He's good at faking and could move under a taller player. Wow, I kept thinking, this was going to be a lot of fun.

"The number 4 position is the *power forward* who will get the closest to the basket and shoot mid-range, jump shots, and close shots to the basket."

Gosh, I thought my brother Johnny would be the one for this position. He's taller than Michael, Marco, or me, and he can do jump shots and move close to the basket. He'd done it a million times when he took a jump shot to get past Frank or Bobby when we played on the streets.

"The number 5 position is the *center*. The *center* is the tallest player on the team. Frank and Bobby are the tallest. They will be in that position. The center's job was to go after each rebound and to defend shooters," he explained. "Only five players are allowed to play, so the other players will be on the bench and go in to relieve any one of you."

After explaining each position that first practice, he placed us in one of them, emphasizing the importance of learning your position as well as the other positions.

We were flabbergasted and did a lot of groaning. Learning all the positions was like going to school—not playing like we did in the streets.

He could see we were overwhelmed. Not deterred, he continued to encourage us. He appealed to our playing the game right, having fun with each other, he suggested, and how proud we would be winning games and maybe even the county championship.

The mention of pride in winning resonated with all of us, but more so with Johnny and I. We wanted so much to make Mom proud of us and being on this team would help us do that. Mr. Sollazzo pledged to us that he would be there every step of the way and at every game. He kept that commitment the entire season.

And practice we did, learning each position. Finally, at the end of the last practice, before our first game, Mr. Sollazzo went to his office and came back with three large cartons. He broke them open and pulled out blue and gold basketball uniforms. He laid them out on a table. The name *Knickerbockers* was written in gold across the chest of the shirts and the numbers were on the back. The shorts had a gold stripe from the hip line on the side. None of us ever expected getting real basketball uniforms. As he called out our names, one by one we went up to get our very own uniform. None us ran to get the uniform; we just walked up slowly and with respect to our coach.

When he handed me my uniform, I moved my hands across the letters, touching them in disbelief that I had a real uniform, that I was a part of a team. I was so proud of myself and all of us. I was thinking at that that I wished I had a father who could be there to see me and Johnny; how proud he would be. And then I looked up at my brother as he accepted his uniform and saw his proud smile. And I knew at that point that I would always remember this one occasion as one of the most important of our lives.

Mr. Solazzo wanted us to be one hell of a basketball team. He trained us so that we could fill those positions interchangeably, causing our opponents to be off guard never knowing what position we would play when we alternated during the game. We went on to win first place in the county and traveled to the regional finals for the championship. The recreation commission and our neighborhood were proud and pleasantly surprised by our undefeated record. In the county championship, we faced a team from White Plains that we beat in the regular season.

It was such a memorable gam. The game went toe to toe , neither team having a score advantage until the last minute of the game. The opposing team scored. Their power forward made a lay-up, taking the lead over us by one point. With sixty seconds on the clock, Michael and I took the ball downcourt. Crossing the center line, Michael passed to me. Marco broke to the foul line with hands open, signaling to me to pass, which I did. He caught it and pivoted to his right, passing to my brother Johnny who caught it. Twenty seconds left, Johnny faked a jump shot and passed the ball to Frank who was under the basket. Ten seconds left, Frank caught the ball, moved from under the basket, and pushed the ball up for a rebound shot to the basket. The ball bounced off the backboard, dropping toward the basket; it caught the rim and spun out of the basket, tumbling to left of Frank. Five seconds left. Frank grabbed the ball and was about to shoot when the buzzer went off, ending the game. Game over.

Frank turned toward his father misreading his father response as disappointment instead of empathy for the team loss. He collapsed in tears, looked up at his father and the team, and said, "I should have made the basket!" Defeat was etched in his voice, and he bowed his head as if in shame. That would stay with Frank the rest of his life.

Unfortunately, we didn't win the regionals. That one point devastated us. We all broke down into tears and moved toward Frank, letting him know it was not his fault.

After we had our cry, Mr. Sollazzo came over, and with a consoling voice, praised us for the effort we made all season and during that last game. As he spoke, our tears subsided, and I began to feel good about what all of us accomplished. Here was Mr. Sollazzo praising us when we lost the most important game of the season, encouraging us to continue to play, and reminding us that there would be other opportunities. I wished my mother had come to this game to see us play. But Mom really had no interest in sports. I understood that. Still I wished that someone, even my older brother Sonny or anyone from my father's family, would have come to see what Johnny and I accomplished. But no one was there to see us at this game or any of the games during the season. Most of all, I wished my father was there.

> *Another lesson taught by Mr. Sollazzo in that in spite of losing and feeling despondent we must rise above our feelings if we are to continue on life's journey. Mr. Solllazzo unselfishly gave to my brother and me by instilling confidence in us through sports and social interaction with others at the Aranac.*

SEVENTEEN

"HEY, ANTHONY, WHAT DID YOU GET?"

Thanksgiving and Christmas recesses interrupted our daily gatherings. Every major holiday, my family would trek off to Brooklyn, New York, to visit our maternal grandmother. There we would have a family gathering with my mother's family. We traveled by the New York, New Haven, and Hartford Railroad to Grand Central Terminal. I would grab a seat by the window on the train ride to New York City. The whole time of the train ride, my brothers and mother would be talking, but I kept looking out the window, watching the people get on the train at each stop or reading the billboards that advertised Broadway plays, cigarettes, and cars. Sometimes I would get a treat when we passed a billboard where the billboard worker would be pasting sheets of the new advertisement. As the train approached the tunnel to Grand Central, daylight turned to night, giving an eerie feeling that the outside world was disappearing. Only the light reflecting off the tracks and silhouettes of the tunnel support arches were visible.

When we got to Grand Central, I was in awe, the movement of thousands of people, scurrying about like ants on an ant hill, as Mom held my hand tightly. As we walked to the IRT subway line, I would stare at the giant Kodak photo display in the center of the station. My mother would pull me as I craned my head upwards, gazing at the green and gold Celestial Ceiling displaying the constellation's stars shaped into the names of each.

From Grand Central, we took the subway to Grandma's apartment. The train and subway ride were always an adventure.

The ride on the subway, with more people in one car than I saw in a week, crushed against one another, their bodies rhythmically brushing against each other with each lurch. When we got to 14th Street, we changed over to the Flushing Avenue line. Mom always had us stand on the platform section that was a movable plate extender. When the train stopped at the station, the plate moved flush to the cars. I didn't trust it, I thought it would move when went got to step into the car. So, when the doors opened, I pulled my mother as hard as I could to get into the car. She laughed the whole time, bending over and whispering to me when we got on, "What are you afraid of? I'm here. Don't worry." But all I could think of was the possibility of my leg getting left behind because the plate chopped it off.

The most joyous holiday of the Christian calendar, Christmas, was the one holiday that my brothers and I dreaded the most, the one when we felt most alone. For sure, I know it was the toughest for my mother.

We traveled to Brooklyn the day after Christmas and came home the day before New Year's. To get enough money for train and subway fare and to help my grandmother with the food expenses, Mom would make wreaths. She asked my brothers and I to go see the vendors who were selling Christmas trees and ask them for branches cut from trees when they were sold to the customers. I always felt hesitant about asking, fearing rejection and embarrassment, especially if my friends saw me. It was like we were beggars. We would go to the lots after supper, hoping no one would see us. There was a bonus I did enjoy—the pine scent from the trees leaning against a rope and the overhead string of light bulbs bringing to life a lot that was barren before.

The vendors were very charitable. They knew our situation and always gave us the spare branches, therefore denying themselves the opportunity to make and sell wreaths. Many times, they also gave us the red berries. Handling the branches would always leave a sappy residue on my hands and clothes. I hated the sticky feeling. Then we would take wire clothes hangers and shape them to form a wreath, tie the branches with a thin wire and interspersing red berries and a red bow. When finished, Sonny went out and sold them. Then on Christmas Eve, when the vendors had a few trees left, we would go and ask them for one. True to their charitable ways, they would always give us one.

When we got the tree home, we decorated it with tinsel and the bulbs and strings of light, as well as all the ornaments Mom had bought when my father was alive. Christmas Eve was probably the hardest. Mom would do her best to try to lift our spirits. She would talk about the importance of Christmas: Christmas was about Christ's birth and all the good He brought to the world. That we should be thankful for a roof over our heads and food on the table. Above all, we should be thankful for each other and always care for one another.

Typically, she made a special dinner—spaghetti with olives and red gravy, Italian bread, and escarole with anchovies and more olives. Mom was a great cook but not a good baker. Her homemade dessert was a cookie covered with a glaze of sugar. Johnny and I used to tease her by claiming that they were rocks. When you bit into one, you heard a massive crunch. Fortunately, Mom made coffee and we dunked them.

It was a simple dinner, which was fine because we knew that a festive meal awaited us in Brooklyn.

When we were younger, and we got up on Christmas morning, Johnny and I would stand before the tree trying to comprehend why nothing was there for us. We knew Mom could not afford to buy us a gift, but what about Santa Claus? After all, I had written to him, carefully addressing my letter to Santa Claus, North Pole, Alaska, and imploring him to send all of us some gifts. Was it because we weren't good? But Santa would not even give a reason.

We hoped that my father's family would at least come to visit with us. It was such a feeling of abandonment. The only time I ever remember anyone from my father's family coming to visit with us on Christmas was when my grandfather surprised us one Christmas Eve when I was about eight years old. The knock on the door startled us. Johnny and I thought maybe, just maybe there was a Santa Clause and maybe he was here that night. When Mom opened the door, there was Grandpa. His silver white hair caught us off guard. We thought it was really Santa Claus standing there with a smile and a package. When he came inside, he handed the package to us and said, "*Buon Natale.*" He was smiling as he watched us open the gift. It was two six shooters and a leather holster. Johnny and I grabbed the guns and started shooting each other, while grandpa laughed the entire time.

> *For Sonny, there was no gift. I often wonder to this day how he felt.*

Grandpa stayed for about a half hour and then left. That was the last time anyone in my father's family ever came at Christmas. It was pretty much that way all year. Whenever my father's family gathered for holidays or family events, we were conspicuously absent. Except for my Aunt Rosie, Aunt Josie, and Uncle Joe who checked on us once in a while, it seemed everyone in my father's family abandoned us after he died.

> *When I look back as to why they did not visit, especially during Christmas, it was probably because they had financial limitations and felt embarrassed that they could not help us. Times*

were tough after World War II as the country was slowly got back on its feet. As we got older (in our adult years), we were more inclusive going to family gatherings.

There was one other Christmas Eve when Johnny and I received a gift. My brother Sonny used the money he earned from caddying and bought us a tin lithographed windup roller coaster set. The exterior had a lithograph painting of people enjoying an amusement park or purchasing food at a concession stand. It came with two windup cars. Johnny and I would play with that toy for hours, watching the cars move over the curving tracks, as my brother Sonny and our Mom were enjoying the happiness we felt.

Now on my mother's side of the family, it was the complete opposite. When we got to Brooklyn, Grandma was thrilled. She lived with my mother's cousin Anna. Grandma lived in a four-story firetrap wood-framed building on Ellery Street. It had no heat other than what came from a wood stove in the kitchen. She had very few material possessions. Anna was taking care of her financially. Her apartment only had three rooms, a kitchen, and two bedrooms with no bathroom. The rooms were called "railroad rooms," one leading into the other in a straight line like a railroad track. For the bathroom, you had to use a common one that was shared with the apartment tenants on the opposite side of the center hallway.

I remember the first time using the common bathroom. When we got to Grandmas after a long day using the trains and subway, my bladder was about to burst. And the first thing I said to her was, "Grandma, Grandma, *dov'e bangno?*"

With a smile, she pointed to a door on which the top part had frosted glass.

I ran, opened the door, saw the toilet, and began to relieve myself. Then, I looked up at the tin ceiling, my eyes wandered to the tub on my left. I gasped. In the tub, there was a dead fish about eighteen inches, with no head, soaking in water. Upset and frightened, I forced myself to release faster, wanting to get out of the bathroom. I rushed outside and yelled, "Mommy! Grandma, there's a dead fish in the bathtub!"

Grandma and Mom burst into a robust laughter. I shoved my hands in my pockets upset that they were laughing. Mom came over to me. "Anthony, the fish in the bathtub is cod. Grandma put it there in the water to soften it. Tonight, she is going to make a fish delicacy called *baccala*. It will have olives and olive oil. We will have a little before supper. You will like it."

That night I just could not bring myself to eat the *baccala*. All I could see was a dead fish in a bathtub.

> *As I got older each time baccala was offered during the holidays*
> *I would still always see that dead fish.*

Christmas at Grandma's was always a pleasant. Grandma made a sauce that whet our appetites. We would feast on turkey, ravioli, braciola, meatballs, and greens, followed by some of these Italian desserts: *Cannoli* filled with sumptuous creamy ricotta, or *Neapolitan Ice Cream*, or *Pizza Fritte* (fried dough covered with confectionary sugar), or Struffoli known as "Honey Balls" (a Neapolitan dish of deep-fried balls of sweet dough covered with honey and sugar sprinkles). These were just a few of the desserts. There was wine for the adults and Coca Cola for the children. Grandma loved giving me a bottle of Coca Cola. She would smile and watch me chug it down non-stop, amazed that it did not burn my throat

The highlight of the visit was when my mother's brother, Uncle Jack, and his wife, Aunt Kitty Confusione, with their daughters, Marie and Delores, and Lucy and Tony Massaro came. Their conversations were a mix of English and Italian. Usually when the conversations burst into a chorus of laughter something was said in Italian so that my brothers and I could not understand what they were laughing about. But we laughed with them anyway. We could feel the genuine warmth and love from them. Uncle Jack and Aunt Kitty never forgot us at Christmas. They would always have gifts for me and my brothers. They always cared about us even visiting us for a few days in the summer. My cousin Marie with her radiant smile, would play with us tossing us into the air as we landed on the bed. One time, she tossed my brother Sonny in the air and he missed the bed, and broke his nose when he hit the floor. The smile turned to despair as the blood oozed out. As they got older each time they saw each other they would laugh about it.

Going back to school after Christmas was just as hard as Christmas Eve. Everybody compared the gifts they got. "I got this", or "I got that," with a litany of gifts as though they just emptied a department store.

When they got to me. "Hey, Anthony, what did you get?"

I would pause, thinking about response. "We went to Brooklyn! Traveled the train and subway. Saw thousands of people. Had great meals with my relatives. And got toys and clothes from our Uncle Jack and Aunt Kitty." I never mentioned the number of gifts, which most times was only two.

Their response was usually, "Wow," sparing me the pain of defining what little number of gifts I actually received.

But really they wanted to hear more about the train rides and the city; most of them never traveled beyond the town limits.

> Our friends in the Purdy Street Gang never asked us what we got for Christmas. They knew what the answer would be.

EIGHTEEN

"YOU'RE LYING TO US. WHAT IS GOING ON?"

New Year's Eve, 1952, was celebrated by sitting around the kitchen table listening to music by Guy Lombardo and his Royal Canadians. Mom would prepare her hard-as-rock cookie treats coated with a sugar glaze; honey balls sprinkled with red, white, and green sugar dots, and Canada Dry Ginger Ale. When the clock struck twelve, Guy Lombardo and his Royal Canadians would play "Auld Lang Syne." My brothers and I would fill our glasses with the Canada Dry ginger ale, raise them as if to salute, and in unison, we'd say, "Happy New Year, Mom," which always brought tears, releasing memories of past times good and bad. Once "Auld Lang Syne" was over, and the music that followed was more upbeat. I would dance with Mom and watch as her reflective smile turned to one of joy.

The year was shaping up to be a very good one. In the spring, with the end of the basketball season, the Aranac and County Organizations honored the league winners. The awards night was well attended by parents. Our team, the Knickerbockers, received two trophies: A gold one for winning the town basketball title and a silver one for coming in second place on the county title. It was a proud time for all of us on the team. Each player was called up to receive his award. As we got the awards, the parents would clap. They clapped for all the players. When Johnny and I went up, it was with mixed emotions. Looking out at the crowd, no one was there from our family to see us receive the award.

The proud feeling for Johnny and me was the holding the trophies. No one from our family was there to congratulate us. We proudly brought the trophies home to show Mom. She never really had an interest in sports; she would just acknowledge that something honorable happened, but then went on with whatever she was doing at the time. I don't think she ever realized how important it was for Johnny and me.

> In 1988, Mom was in her last year of life and living with us. Unable to move about and confined to a chair, she watched The Summer Olympics, trying to understand all the different sports including baseball. She finally came to understand them and why people had such an interest. It was then that I realized why she did not have an interest in understanding sports when we were young. She didn't have the time to enjoy leisure activities. She was too busy trying to survive and bring us up. The boy in me felt so much better.

In May, Blackie. our beloved dog. passed away. We all felt a void with his passing. In the summer, Mr. Sollazzo got me to play on the Cardinals Little League baseball team. The rest of the summer passed pretty much like the summers before, but with much less mischievous activity as the lessons of the fort were a reminder to curtail our daring adventurous pursuits.

That fall, I was entering the fifth grade. I did not like my fifth grade teacher, and I'm sure he did not like me. I think he knew what happened with the fort and kept a wary eye on me, waiting for opportune times to correct me, especially when I would whisper to a classmate while he was giving a lesson. Most times when other classmates did the same, he gave them a pass.

> I still have a photo of my fifth grade class taken in October 1952. What strikes me about the photo is that all the class-mates had genuine smiles. Our teacher is standing behind me, hands folded, smiling. My smile is restrained because I felt un-comfortable with him behind me.

When we went to Brooklyn for the holidays, Mom surprised us. The day before we left for home, she took my brothers and I for a walk. Stopping outside a pet store window, she turned toward us with a smile. "Which one of those puppy dogs do you like?"

We were so excited and wrapped our arms around her. The void left by Blackie would be filled.

"Go ahead, pick one!"

We looked in the window, and there in the corner was a beautiful light brown and black hair mixed-breed with dominant German Shepherd genes. We all agreed without exception that he was the dog we wanted.

Mom went inside and bartered with the pet store owner. She pur-chased the dog for $5.00, which could have paid for groceries.

When we got outside, the first question we had was what to name him. Sonny held him and felt his paws, carefully turning and studying them. "You know, judging from the size of his paws, he will be a lot bigger than Blackie. We will name him Rex. He will be the king of all the dogs in the neighborhood." And we agreed with the name.

"Mom, how are we going to take him on the train?" I asked.

"He's small enough to put in a box. No one will know he is in there. It's your job to keep him quiet if he acts up." And that's what we did.

A couple of times on the train ride home, Rex whimpered. The conductor was going seat to seat to punch tickets. He heard the whimper and turned sharply toward us. Johnny and I stuck our hand in the box and pet Rex to calm him. I was looking right into the conductor's eyes and gave him a smile, praying he would not come to our seat. Animals were not allowed on trains, and he could put us off the train at one of the stops. The conductor paused, held the ticket punch and ticket from one of the passengers. He gave me a smile back, and returned to punching tickets. I think he knew what was in the box and looked the other way.

I remember when we got home that Rex was not looking right. He was just lying on the floor not moving. I thought he was sick. We tried to coax him to eat something, but he did not move. I began to get worried. I was praying that he was not dying when suddenly he coughed, gagged, and spit up a huge piece of food.

When Mom went to pick it up, she said, "Look at this. It's a piece of fish! How could that pet owner feed that to a dog? If I were in front of him now, I would give him a piece of my mind!" Well lucky for Rex, because from that day on, whenever we had macaroni and meatballs, she would give him a meatball or two. And for breakfast, he sometimes had eggs and toast. She treated him as one of us.

It seemed that everything was starting to go in the right direction for us as a family. Johnny and I, like all the gang members, were settling down, staying focused on going to Aranac and keeping our mischievous activities to a bare minimum.

Later that week, we all noticed Mom was extremely irritable. I could not figure out what it was that we were doing that made her that way. We were taking care of the dog, playing with Rex in the yard, keeping the house clean, and staying out of trouble.

Finally, I decided to ask my brother Sonny. Because he was the oldest, Mom sometimes confided in him. "What's going on? Why is Mom always mad?"

Sonny would only say, "I don't know! Leave me alone!"

Johnny motioned me to the living room with his forefinger over his lips. He had a knack for finding out things. "Anthony, I don't know what is going on either. But don't keep asking Sonny. You know how he gets when he knows something and can't tell us. He will only get mad at you. And you know how scary that is."

I remembered the time he slapped my face when I objected to cleaning his muskrat traps. "OK, Johnny. I won't ask him, but I don't like what Mom is doing."

It continued day after day. Just before New Year's Day, I couldn't take it anymore. When she returned late one afternoon from supposedly food shopping, I confronted her. "Mom, why are you mad at us? You said you were going shopping, but you don't have any bags of food from the store. You're lying to us. What is going on?"

Then a barrage of tears came raining down her cheeks.

She looked tired. Those dark rings under her eyes looked even darker, her facial features taut. She came over to me and gave me a hug, calming me.

Sitting down at the kitchen table, bringing me with her, she motioned to Sonny and Johnny to join us. She looked so downtrodden. Something had stolen her spirit. Then she began to tell us. "The landlord sold our home. As renters, we have to find a new home. I have been out looking for a new place in town for a couple of months. I tried so hard to rent a home in town, but the rents are too high, or the landlords don't want children. There is nothing near here. Even Aunt Rosie and Uncle

Joe went looking for us. I tried to have the new owners give us until June so all of you could finish school. But the new owners want to move into our home before the end of January. I'm sorry, but we have to move to a city. We have no choice. I could only afford the rent for a home in New Rochelle. I know it will be hard for you to not be going to the same school or seeing your friends. I know how close all of you are with the other boys. But we have no choice."

My whole world collapsed like a sandcastle swept away by waves. I cried, "Mom, I don't want to move! I want to stay here! Let's stop them from making us move! We have rights!"

Mom smiled a little with the fervor of my self-righteousness. "Anthony, no, we can't do that. It's the law, and the people that bought the house have the right to it."

But Sonny was angry—the angriest I'd ever seen him. He turned toward Mom. "I'm not going to finish high school in a city where I don't know anyone! I'll live with Grandma in Harrison and finish my high school here. I'm not going."

Mom turned to us again. "I know how fearful you must be. I left Italy at ten years old, leaving my friends and the small town of Maddaloni to settle in Brooklyn. My mother and I felt then as I do today, not knowing what to expect in a new country. Once we left, that was it. We knew we could never go back. But I met new friends, learned a new language, and went on to learn a trade as a seamstress. At least, you will have the chance to come back here to visit your friends. They are your friends now, and they will always be your friends. Only God knows why we have to do this. But knowing what He has done for me over the years, it will all work out. We'll get past this."

"No, we won't!" was Sonny's response, and he stormed out of the house, slamming the door so hard the windowpanes on it shook.

The biggest devastation was to my mother. The bloodshot eyes and dark rings under them displayed her agony. She had to move from the home she once owned but lost when my father died. She was distraught that she couldn't stay in the home she loved or bring us up in the town we loved.

And so, we went from a small town to a city of 70,000. It was a move away from the friends we loved as brothers and was heartbreaking to us. We felt helpless. Our lives suddenly turned upside down. We were fearful of what awaited us in New Rochelle.

When we moved, Mom got a job as a seamstress, finally working again, throwing the shackles of county assistance away forever. But there was a cost for the move. My brother Sonny had reluctantly moved with us and his constant anger made the move more difficult for all of us. He went to the new high school for one week but didn't try to make friends in the new high school. He wanted to be with his friends back in Harrison. Not a day passed in that first week that he didn't have an outburst of anger. He was unbearable. Finally, my mother could not endure his constant temper. She capitulated and let him move in with my grandmother in Harrison, so he could finish high school there. She was deeply hurt by his leaving. Our family was being broken up.

The move inflicted a heavy toll on Johnny and I, too, as we adjusted to a new environment. Of course, we wished we could return to Harrison, like Sonny did, but we were younger and could not leave Mom.

We missed the gang—the friendship as well as the escapades we shared with them: Our exploits with the fort instilled in us a discipline of persistence in achieving goals that might seem impossible. The camaraderie with Michael, Marco, Frank, and Bobby established the meaning of loyalty, trust, respect, and teamwork. It was a time when we made do with virtually nothing. We didn't even know we were poor. We enjoyed every day as an adventure. Necessity was (as the saying goes) the mother of invention. It also gave us the opportunity to experience the compassion of others like Mr. Sollazzo, Mr. Marshall, Mrs. Patterson, and Mr. Fiore who took an interest in channeling our energies to a positive outcome, showing us what a person can do with the right guidance.

Lost into a new time and place, forever creating a chasm between the past and future, our interactions with the gang slowly slipped away, and the maturity of growing up in New Rochelle and the distance between it and Harrison broke the physical bond. But the fort and all the other adventures still lived in each of us as the ultimate true friendship.

> *Often my thoughts turn to the days when my brother Johnny and I had to be on our own without the Purdy Street Gang as support. New Rochelle was daunting at first. I would soon be twelve, and Johnny was fourteen. In a new city, we had to as-similate fast. Despite the loss of the gang, Johnny continued to always egg me on to do the impossible. Over the years, that prepared me for challenges.*

> *The result was a new set of adventures even more challenging than the earlier ones in Harrison, New York. But that's a story yet to be told.*

NINETEEN

"IT WAS A GREAT TIME. WE WERE LUCKY."

My goal when I first started this novel was to share with all of my childhood friends and my brothers the stories of our daring and mischievous younger years. I wanted to have them feel that sense of adventure one more time as they share these tales with their families, and every once in a while, smile as they look back at the boy in them that they once were.

I reached out to Frank and Bobby Sollazzo, Marco, Michael, and Jerry Bisceglia, and my brothers Michael (Sonny) and Johnny. Reconnecting with my childhood friends was a rewarding and emotional experience, reliving the days of a carefree youth. It was rewarding that, after many years, I was able to see them one more time.

Three of those visits are especially memorable.

Frank Sollazzo

The year was 2010. I went to Harrison to take photos of most of the locations mentioned in this novel. I decided that day to go to Frank's house and, hopefully, chat with him. It was a meaningful visit. I went to the Frank P. Sollazzo Recreation Center— named for Frank's father—to find out if Frank was still living in town. They gave me his address; the good news was that he lived only a block away from where we built our fort. But they warned me to approach him carefully. Times were not the best for him.

Walking up to his front door, I started to get butterflies in my stomach, not knowing what to expect or how Frank would react. I approached the front door very cautiously. I knocked on the door, and then stood back from it.

"Who's there?" came a strong hostile response.

I asked, "Is this Frank Sollazzo's residence?" In that instant, I realized that I made matters worse by the way I asked.

"Yea, it is! And who wants to know?"

I could hear him walking to the door. So, I had to think fast. "Frank, it's Anthony Matero from Parsons Street."

I waited what seemed to be an hour before the door opened.

Frank stood there in the doorway, towering over me. God, I thought, his features have not changed that much. I recognized him immediately.

But he was looking me over, too, not readily recognizing me. Then he said, "Jesus Christ, what the hell happened to you, Anthony?"

I cracked up laughing. "Frank, what the hell do you expect after fifty-six years? I got old like all of us. How the hell are you?"

We both laughed.

Frank invited me in, and we chatted for almost an hour about the fort and that memorable basketball game. He told me that he never forgot that game. It still lingered with him like it does with me. To this day, when he thinks about the lost championship, he feels he let everyone down. He told me that he so wanted that game to be one where everyone would be proud of him. He was disappointed that he could not make the basket for us to win the game.

Then he turned to me. "Anthony, it was nice seeing you today. I often thought about you and your brothers and how what happened to you was so unfair when you had to move. I really enjoyed growing up with all the guys in our neighborhood. It was a great time. We were lucky. Say hello to your brother Johnny for me."

"Frank, before I leave, let me take a picture to send to Johnny. I'm sure he will be happy to see you."

Frank smiled and, while I took the picture, he jested. "Tell Johnny I'm sending my regards." And just before I clicked the photo, he raised his hand, index finger pointing up, busting Johnny's chops as he always did.

I laughed and said, "Frankie, nothing's changed." We shook hands, and I left.

As I drove away, I waved to him, and he just stood there looking at me. I wondered what he was thinking.

Marco

Then I made contact with Marco and eventually we were able to get together. This was around 2011. Marco was living in Florida. I called him to let him know we were visiting relatives there. Marco thought it would be great to get together and relive the old days. He invited us to stay with him and his wife Barbara. His brother, Michael, also was living in Florida.

The visit was memorable. Marco had Michael over for dinner the night we arrived to visit with them. All we talked about were the incidents in this novel. Our laughter bounced off the walls, especially the night of the battle. But Michael was suffering from Alzheimer's, and it was sad to see him grasping for the memories. Even though this was a happy time, my heart sank each time Michael looked at me, recognizing me for a brief second and then the look of trying to determine where he met me.

Bisceligia

In 2013, two years later, the brothers Bisceligia and Matero met at Risoli's restaurant on Purdy Street in Harrison, New York. It was a memorable and sobering reunion: Memorable because it was the first time we were all together since our leaving Harrison, yet sobering because Michael Alzheimer's was getting worse. Jerry and Marco cautiously watched him as we sat for lunch. Michael kept getting up and moving around, wanting to walk away.

Memories are such a precious gift. That I wanted to share them was the primary goal of this memoir with my friends and brothers. Time, however, can rob you of that. Marco often times in our phone conversations would ask, "When are you going to finish the novel? Better hurry up; time is not on our side." He was so right. I wish that the novel was finished after that last and final meeting with Marco and his brothers so it could have been shared with every one of them. Since that time, my brother Michael (Sonny), Jerry, Marco, and Michael Bisceglia, as well as Frank Sollazo have passed—Marco and Frank as recently as the month before my completing this novel, as did all the friends that built that lopsided boat in Jerry Bisceglia's basement. The Biltmore Movie Theater and the park by the railroad station are gone. Soon to be replaced by condominiums.

There are only three of us left now—My brother Johnny, me, and Bobby Sollazzo. I can't cry at the passing of others because my heart tells me they are alive and, in another dimension, perhaps a better one I hope. This memoir is a living tribute to their adventures and companionship and a time when the word "free" truly meant to act and live as one wishes.

ACKNOWLEDGEMENTS

I am most grateful for the words of encouragement and input from each of the following family, friends, and colleagues, as well as their patience while I wrote and rewrote this novel. Without their support, this book would never have happened.

Barbara Bisceglia

Lucille Kaye

Peggy Harrington

Bobby Guerierie

Sue Nesin

I am also thankful for advice and guidance from members of the Rehoboth Beach Writers Guild:

Maribeth Fischer, author and founder of the Guild, who encouraged me over the years to persevere in writing this story

Nancy P. Sherman, author, copy editor, and "Coffee & Chat" leader

Tom Hoyer, leader of the Wednesday night "Free Writes"

John Lester, author and architect, for his help in recreating the fort image as a guide for the cover artist

CPSIA information can be obtained
at www.ICGtesting.com
Printed in the USA
LVHW011256191220
674520LV00004B/461